Providing quality care in a compassionate and efficient manner is the goal of every healthcare provider. But how can this lofty goal be achieved? Read One Patient at a Time *and adopt the principles and philosophies presented, and you will have your answer. This book will empower you to do your best. It worked for me!*

—David K. Talley, OD, FAAO

Managing Partner, West Tennessee Eye, PLLC

In today's fast-paced world, when attention spans are short, it is easy to get caught up in a frenzy of sameness. How do you differentiate your business? There is still a place for independent success when you combine single interactions and business acumen. The Kegarises share their insights and lead by example to help today's optometrist find success!

—Carol L. Alexander, OD, FAAO

Head, North America Vision Care Professional Relations
Johnson and Johnson Vision

—Kevin L. Alexander, OD, PhD, FAAO

President, Marshall B. Ketchum University

When I was asked by Jeff and Susan Kegarise to endorse their book One Patient at a Time, *I stopped to reflect on my personal and business experience with the authors. For many years, I was in the position to personally see Jeff and Susan put into practice what they have so eloquently described in their book. In an age of increasing regulations, computerization, and technology-driven care, they have identified the essential ingredients required for a successful healthcare practice. Their focus on service and putting the relationship with the patient as a main priority speaks volumes to their success. I encourage any individual in business, healthcare or not, to read this book. New healthcare practitioners would value the insights and directions contained in this book, throughout their careers. Perhaps a new requirement in future practice management courses. An excellent compilation of successful service-driven techniques and insights so necessary in today's advancing technology. A reminder that patients (customers) are human beings drawn to those who deliver personal care and service—something that will never change.*

—Randall N. Reichle, OD, FAAO

Diplomate, American Board of Optometry
Eye Center of Texas

ONE PATIENT AT A TIME

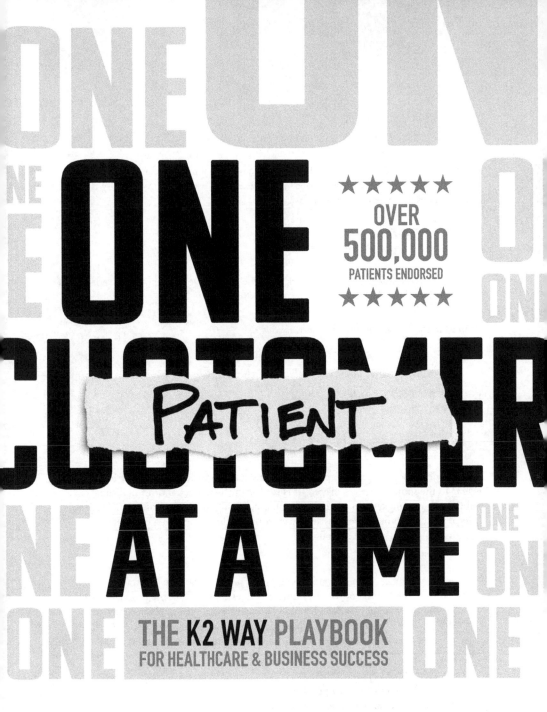

ONE CUSTOMER PATIENT AT A TIME

★★★★★
OVER
500,000
PATIENTS ENDORSED
★★★★★

THE K2 WAY PLAYBOOK
FOR HEALTHCARE & BUSINESS SUCCESS

DRS. JEFF & SUSAN KEGARISE

Advantage

Published by Advantage, Charleston, South Carolina.
Member of Advantage Media Group.

ADVANTAGE is a registered trademark, and the Advantage colophon is a trademark of Advantage Media Group, Inc.

Printed in the United States of America.

10 9 8 7 6 5 4 3 2 1

ISBN: 978-1-64225-154-8
LCCN: 2020902245

Cover and layout design by David Taylor.

This publication is designed to provide accurate and authoritative information in regard to the subject matter covered. It is sold with the understanding that the publisher is not engaged in rendering legal, accounting, or other professional services. If legal advice or other expert assistance is required, the services of a competent professional person should be sought.

Advantage Media Group is proud to be a part of the Tree Neutral® program. Tree Neutral offsets the number of trees consumed in the production and printing of this book by taking proactive steps such as planting trees in direct proportion to the number of trees used to print books. To learn more about Tree Neutral, please visit www.treeneutral.com.

Advantage Media Group is a publisher of business, self-improvement, and professional development books and online learning. We help entrepreneurs, business leaders, and professionals share their Stories, Passion, and Knowledge to help others Learn & Grow. Do you have a manuscript or book idea that you would like us to consider for publishing? Please visit advantagefamily.com or call 1.866.775.1696.

DEDICATIONS

Dr. Jeff

To my parents, Ron and Ann Kegarise.

To my mom, your positive attitude, love of life, and tenacity taught me the ways to be compassionate, loving, and caring.

To my dad, for sharing your wisdom and introducing me to quality improvement and its vast ramifications for improving healthcare. You are the best father and business consultant I could ever have.

Dr. Susan

To my parents, Cherry and Lloyd, whose love, values, and integrity live within and guide me daily. Your wisdom and support made me feel I could be or do anything I wanted. It is an honor to be your daughter.

Both

To our children, Christen, Kevin, and Kelli, for joining us on late-night "adventures" at the office while we worked to improve our care and businesses. Thanks for tolerating our teaching of service (okay, occasionally preaching!). We are so proud that each of you demonstrate the personal behaviors of caring, courteousness, and service in your treatment of others.

To Susan from Jeff

With the help of the editors, I am sneaking this appreciation message in.

This book is a compilation of both your and my beliefs. And you, more than any doctor I have ever seen, met, or consulted with, demonstrate a true love for the patients in your care.

The authenticity in your love of people and your boundless energy has been shown as a woman who has successfully balanced being a mother, wife, and business owner. For every lesson we espouse, you are the role model.

For every success I personally may have had, you are truly the wind beneath my wings.

For every day I live, you make life a great experience.

I love you.

CONTENTS

PREFACE xix

Why We Wrote This Book

INTRODUCTION .1

The Vision

CHAPTER 1 5

Focus on the Patient's Care and Experience

Lesson 1: Putting Patients First

Lesson 2: Answering the Phone Is an Opportunity

Lesson 3: Smile When You Say That

Lesson 4: Greet Everyone with a Smile and Make Eye Contact

Lesson 5: Welcome to the Office!

Lesson 6: It's a Reception Area

Lesson 7: You Do a Lot—Make Sure Your Patients Know It

Lesson 8: Greeting the Patient IN the Reception Room

Lesson 9: Help Me Up So I Don't Go Down

Lesson 10: Have Someone in Charge of Care

Lesson 11: Wait, Don't Walk So Far and So Fast

Lesson 12: A Conjunctivitis Did Not Just Walk in the Door

Lesson 13: I Can Hear You—Why Aren't You Taking Care of Me?

Lesson 14: Personal Info Is as Important as Medical Info

Lesson 15: Shhh—Use Soft-Touch Keyboards

Lesson 16: Duck! And Don't Slam the Door

Lesson 17: Education Is a Part of Care

Lesson 18: Certainty Is More Valued Than Uncertainty

Lesson 19: And I Would Do Anything for You, But I Can't Do That

Lesson 20: Change Is Good If You Give It First

Lesson 21: At Y(our) Service

Lesson 22: Proud to Be an American

Lesson 23: I Will Show You to the Bathroom and Back

Lesson 24: Murphy's Law of Clinical Care

Lesson 25: Double Take

Lesson 26: Doctors Should Make House Calls

Lesson 27: Honesty Is the Best Policy

Lesson 28: Provide Charitable Care—Internally

Lesson 29: New Patient Cards and Personalized Notes

Lesson 30: Even If You Leave, You Are Always Welcome Here

Lesson 31: Thanksgiving with Patients

Lesson 32: Transferring and Receiving a Call—Rinse and Repeat

Lesson 33: Smile for the Camera

Lesson 34: $10-$10-$100 Making Smiles (Yours and Theirs)

CHAPTER 2 . . . . **57**

Focus on Leadership and Strategy

Lesson 35: Look in the Mirror

Lesson 36: The Mission Must Live!

Lesson 37: One Mission, Five Important Goals

Lesson 38: We Believe in BBs

Lesson 39: Strategy Is a Process, Not an Event

Lesson 40: The Annual Strategic Review

Lesson 41: Laminated Yearly Goal Cards

Lesson 42: Minimize "Staff Infections" by Having Good Staff Meetings

Lesson 43: Have a Staff Meeting Once a Week, and Always Train

Lesson 44: Staff Meeting Notebooks

Lesson 45: The Empty Chair Speaks Loudest

Lesson 46: Pick a Patient of the Week Every Week

Lesson 47: Staff Meeting Thank-Yous—Appreciation Notes

Lesson 48: WOWs

Lesson 49: Stick Your Neck Out Award

Lesson 50: Crazy Antics Say It's Okay to Do Crazy Good Things

Lesson 51: Fire Up! Ten, Nine, Eight …

Lesson 52: What We're Afraid Of

Lesson 53: Do Not Open the Door—until We're Ready

Lesson 54: The Gap—and I'm Not Talking Jeans

CHAPTER 3 . . . . **89**

Focus on Management: Reinforcing the View

*Lesson 55: You May Never Know All the Facts,
but You Still Have to Make a Decision*

Lesson 56: Sometimes the Best Decision Is No Decision

Lesson 57: Good Enough to Act

*Lesson 58: Think Not What Your Patients Can Do for
You but What More You Can Do for Your Patients*

*Lesson 59: Don't Use Cruise Control When You're
Driving Downhill—There's a Truck on Your Tail*

Lesson 60: The Lost World—Laugh at the Scary Parts

Lesson 61: Accelerated Benchmarking—Outside Healthcare

Lesson 62: Accelerated Benchmarking—Disney-esque Hierarchy

Lesson 63: Never Apologize for Fees

Lesson 64: Name's on the Door!

Lesson 65: How You See Is as Important as What You Say

Lesson 66: We're Still Learning. Are You?

Lesson 67: Once-a-Year Testing

Lesson 68: He Takes a Shot and Scores!

Lesson 69: Urban Meyer Units—As You Grow, Stay Small

Lesson 70: Heads Up—Make It Visible

Lesson 71: It's Getting Hot in Here

Lesson 72: We Are in It for the Money—at Least Partially

CHAPTER 4 . . . . **125**

Focus on Developing, Building, and Nurturing a Culture

Lesson 73: You Just Have to Demonstrate

Lesson 74: What We're Not Afraid Of

Lesson 75: Be Proud of the Appearance of Your Staff

Lesson 76: A Little Personalization Builds a Lot of Relationships

Lesson 77: Lanyards? The Staff Says No

Lesson 78: Show Off Staff Accomplishments—Not Just Doctors'

Lesson 79: You Want to Make What? We Want You to Make More!

Lesson 80: Favorites—We Know What You Like

*Lesson 81: Sometimes You Have to Demonstrate
Over and Over—or Watch Dr. Susan!*

Lesson 82: The First Thing New Staff Members Should Hear

*Lesson 83: We Are Not Closing Today; We Are
Getting Ready to Open Tomorrow*

Lesson 84: Doctors Don't Talk Fees

Lesson 85: We Almost Never Celebrate the Person Who's Leaving

Lesson 86: Moments of Truth in Clinical Care

CHAPTER 5 . . . . **149**

Focus on Our People and Behaviors

Lesson 87: Praise Frequently—but Know When and Where

Lesson 88: Have a PIC NIC

Lesson 89: Don't BS Us, Cuz We Won't BS You

Lesson 90: Don't Take It Personally

Lesson 91: Those Who Trust and Those Who Don't

*Lesson 92: How You Listen and Respond
Is as Important as What You Do*

Lesson 93: And One Reviews

Lesson 94: No Sinner Was Ever Saved with One Sermon

Lesson 95: Your Skills Are Great, Yet We Expect More

Lesson 96: What Is Your Value?

Lesson 97: How Much Do You Weigh?

Lesson 98: You Can't Buy Loyalty

Lesson 99: Firing—Doing What Is Right

Lesson 100: Rehiring Previous Employees

Lesson 101: We've Got Your Back

Lesson 102: The Best They'll Ever Be

*Lesson 103: Don't Be a Jerk, or, How Do They
Handle Being Served Cold Soup?*

Lesson 104: The Kegarise Theory of Relativity on Hiring

Lesson 105: Sleeping with the Owner

Lesson 106: Never Be Completely Satisfied

CHAPTER 6 191

Focus on Systems that Provide Better Service to Patients

Lesson 107: Loyalty Matrix

Lesson 108: Treat the Person First, Then the Process—Recovery

Lesson 109: Pareto-izing Our Recovery Results

Lesson 110: You May Not Be an Owner, Yet You Still Own

Lesson 111: Monthly Loyalty Review

*Lesson 112: Communication Marketing—
Listen, Document, Target*

CHAPTER 7 . . . . **209**

Focus on Efficiency and Effectiveness

Lesson 113: If Your Reception Room Becomes a Waiting Room, That's Inventory

Lesson 114: Don't Balance Capacity with Patient Demand

Lesson 115: The Doctor Should Be Your Constraint

Lesson 116: Active, Not Passive, Systems

Lesson 117: Top Gun—Scribe as Wingman

Lesson 118: More Calls Out Than In

CHAPTER 8 . . . . **221**

Focus on Creating Consistency in Imaging and Marketing

Lesson 119: Fonts and Consistency

Lesson 120: Anything Written Represents Us

Lesson 121: Pet Peeve—Handout Inconsistency

Lesson 122: Laminate for Emphasis

Lesson 123: Our Practice Logo

Lesson 124: Leave a Business Card

Lesson 125: Dressing Our Offices

Lesson 126: It's Cold Outside, Yet We All Dress the Same

Lesson 127: Are You Fully Dressed?

Lesson 128: What's in Your Pocket?

Lesson 129: Develop a Good Relationship with a Nice Restaurant

Lesson 130: My Favorite Restaurant—a Table Full of Notes

Lesson 131: I'll Take a Four Top, Please

Lesson 132: Keeping Up Appearances

Lesson 133: Where to Smoke 'Em If You Have to Have 'Em

Lesson 134: No Front Door Entrance or Exit for Us

Lesson 135: Office Design and NeverLost

CONCLUSION 245

Putting It All Together

ACKNOWLEDGMENTS 249

APPENDIX 251

CONTACT INFORMATION 255

ABOUT THE AUTHORS 257

I immediately recognized this was a top-notch team from the moment I received my first call back.

I came in from out of town with no idea where to go and they got me right in and provided notes for me to follow up with my eye doctor back home. Very helpful!

Cool Springs EyeCare saved me today!

PREFACE
Why We Wrote This Book

Healthcare has changed over the past thirty years—from manually written (scribbled) doctor notes to computerized medical records, protection of patient privacy, electronic submission of medication Rx's, and reconciliation of those meds. But it often seems like algorithm-biased, evidence-based, cookbook medicine driven by doctors, nurses, and caregivers x-ing boxes aimed at satisfying insurance companies and government agencies. We have made gains, yes. Yet we have not seen the promised improvements in efficiency and effectiveness in care so desired by patients and clinicians. We have not witnessed any noticeable improvements in the level of compassion and attention to courteous delivery of care that should be fundamental in health care. No matter your electronic medical record (EMR), chosen specialty, mode of practice, method of delivery, or location of service, one fact remains a constant: healthcare is personal. And it is personal whether it's fee based, capitated, union or non-union, large or small. In the words of Dr. Paul Batalden, it is provided by the single smallest team of people, systems, and patients—a microsystem.

Microsystems are increasingly part of larger, clout-fueled, bottom-line-oriented checker players called *macrosystems*—all fighting each other to expand efficiencies, improve care, and gain market share. You and I know them as the multisite hospital chain provider, the enormously large medical specialty group, or even as the physician practice, each of whom is likely owned and financially backed by a hospital chain or large academic center. As these large centers fight for more control, they become less connected to what is practiced in real-world situations, where a doctor's care is judged by the real customer of care, the patient. As paychecks and egos grow by moving checker pieces, through leveraged buyouts and acquisitions, all aimed at becoming the dominant player in a community, state, or region, the focus on courteous and personal care desired by patients is diminished.

That type of *best in clinical care and patient experience goal* resides less in behemoth corporate-owned healthcare facilities and more with individual providers of care. It is as if, somewhere along the line, everyone forgot that patients *expect* doctors to be well trained and knowledgeable (what Theodore Levitt called the expected product[1]) but judge the care based on concern, empathy, trust, attitude, and courteousness of the care delivery team and its systems (the augmented product).

Clinical care is increasingly evidence-based, and that is a good thing, as long as exceptions to the evidence are understood to occur and managed individually. Systems of care are experientially based. The essence of great care should be defined by the patient when clinical care and clinical services combine to create a differentiated, appreciated, and valued experience.

---

1   Theodore Levitt, "Marketing Myopia," in *HBR's 10 Must Reads on Strategic Marketing*, (Harvard Business Review Press, April 2013).

We believe that no matter where or how long you have practiced, as a doctor, nurse, technician, receptionist, secretary, accounts supervisor, payroll processor, or any position in the healthcare business, service to patients and hospitality is a key part of your job description. Your organization's success should be defined by the level to which you successfully provide this type of care. Yet how can this happen in an era of declining reimbursements, technological disrupters, new legislative regulations, mergers, acquisitions, checklists, paperwork, and extra administrative burdens? One word: leadership.

Leadership defines (or redefines) what great care is. Leadership that trains people, builds systems, innovates to improve, and dedicates itself to great care. Is that easy? Heck no. Is it impossible? Definitely, heck no! Like anything of real value, it is created and accomplished through thousands of short-term interactions and improvements. Many individual moments of truth occur where the customer (patient) is evaluating their care (experience) and forming an opinion. They may seek care often via their insurance plan, yet your goal is that they stay with you and your practice due to loyalty.

It doesn't matter what size your practice is, whether you are in a public, private, or academic setting, we believe strong leadership is imperative. We have witnessed this fact in organizations we have worked with, from as small a microsystem (Donelson EyeCare, circa 1995) to multidoctor, multisite practices. We have insisted upon and demonstrated the value of the leader's focus in even the largest of healthcare entities where we have consulted, lectured, or advised. And you know what? Despite the apparent differences between radiology and optometry, internal medicine and dentistry, emergency medicine and outpatient care, we have found very little difference in the methods and ability to learn and improve the delivery of the service experience to patients. Subtle differences, yes. Fundamental and profound differences, heck no.

Therefore, we felt the need to share this collection of K2 "Kegarise Way" management and patient care methods. It is not so comprehensive that it describes everything we do and have espoused while building our successful eye-care businesses. Yet it is also not so brief that it only touches on a few ideas. What is shared in the book are fundamentals we have learned, practiced, taught, and shared in many settings over the years. If you are a leader who desires the best for your patients (or customers) and employees, these insights have the potential to help you reinforce great care and experience as your cultural norm. When these lessons are carefully studied, employed, and demonstrated by your leaders the potential to dramatically improve the care in medicine, optometry, and healthcare exists, for patients and providers. And is that a really good thing? Heck yes!

This book reflects the passion we have for our eye-care teams and the patients we treat. It is a behind-the-curtain look at how we do what we do and why we have built a reputation (locally, nationally, even internationally) for clinical care and healthcare business management.

While this book started as a "service manual of standards," one of the cornerstones of our culture building, it has grown to help us accomplish the following goals:

1. To act as a catalytic set of fundamentals for other doctors to embrace and emulate. To encourage doctors, nurses, administrators, managers, staff, and healthcare leaders to copy, massage, and improve these methods to deliver the type of care we each want as a patient.

2. To invigorate and encourage doctors who want to build and lead relationship-focused excellence in care to their patients. And to demonstrate that it can be done and done well. To

say to those doctors, challenged and motivated to provide clinical, operational, and innovative care, that you are not alone!

3. To let our existing patients know how much intentional effort we put into delivering and improving the eye-care and care experience delivered at our practices.

4. To remind our patients that we are certain this is the best place to meet their (and their friends, family, and coworkers') vision and eye health needs.

5. To solidify in our team of doctors and staff the fundamental principles, lessons, and expectations we believe are critical to delivering the patient experience we seek.

6. To have our patients reinforce our behaviors by making sure we are walking the talk in providing the care experience promise we seek for every patient, every time.

From the time I walked in until I left, nothing but excellent customer service. I believe bosses set a business environment, and this says volumes about top management as well as the hiring manager. Kudos to the entire staff.

They listen to you and take their time to understand your needs.

Such a friendly place; makes it easy to want to go to the eye doctor!

INTRODUCTION

The Vision

HOW TO USE THIS BOOK

My vision in life is to unite ... as two eyes make one in sight.

—Paraphrase of Robert Frost, "Two Tramps in Mud Time"

The goal of this book is to improve healthcare—specifically, the patient care experience by delivering that care one patient at a time. Its primary focus is on doctors, but it is also written to help patients. The more patients want, expect, and demand from their doctor visit, the better the level of standard care provided will be. We encourage patients to recommend or give a copy of this book to their doctors. It will help the doctor and, as a result, you as their patient.

Most doctors want to provide better care, yet many feel too constrained by the ever-increasing administrative burdens and declining reimbursements—each of which cuts into the time available for patient care. Though we acknowledge that each of these business pressures exist, they are not an excuse for delivering a poor patient experience. "The leader gets what the leader wants."

We have organized this book into easily implementable lessons. This easily readable and digestible method we learned from Harvey MacKay in his book *Swim with the Sharks without Being Eaten Alive*. Pick one or two lessons to focus on and ask yourself or, even better, your staff, "Do we do this?" If not, "Could we, should we?" If yes, "How could we do it better or more consistently?"

You can use these lessons as an overall gauge of your practice, yet we recommend starting with a few individual lessons. By picking a few that are most meaningful to you, they can be monitored and managed as vital signs of your organizational performance.

While individual lessons are great, ultimately, the real power of the book comes from connecting the lessons into an organized approach to leading, managing, culture building, and creating a systems-oriented healthcare practice. That type of practice possesses energized people (staff and doctors) striving to deliver and improve patient care. That office culture is a joyous one in which to work and is fun for patients to visit. Pursuing the goal of a better care experience one patient at a time, each and every visit, can transform your business.

The staff and doctors are great. Best place my family has ever gotten eye care and eyewear from.

Fantastic service. Fantastic staff. Didn't try to upsell. So glad we found this place.

The place was quite busy, but we were in an examining room faster than I've experienced in any other medical facility.

If you need a great eye doctor, this is the place to go.

I was glad that they had an effective alternative to dilating my pupils. I did not have to wait more than a few minutes to be seen. Everyone was courteous and professional.

I felt like I received the most thorough eye exam I had ever gotten.

Best eye-care clinic ever!

CHAPTER 1

Focus on the Patient's Care and Experience

Always do right. This will gratify some people and astonish the rest.

—Mark Twain

This first chapter focuses on what we believe are fundamental deliverables in each and every visit or interaction between our offices and patients. From the first impression (by any technological means available, customized for the patient) to the initial greeting when the patient enters, through the entire visit and including follow-up care, communication, and education, the experience for the patient must be intentionally great.

The following lessons are comprehensive yet by no means represent all of what we do. They reflect what our patients should experience each and every time they interact with us. For all patients (ours and others), we trust and hope these lessons will result in an aha revelation that, yes, that is what I as a patient deserve. I *do* want that type of experience from my doctor and in my healthcare. And, if I'm a doctor, this is the type of experience I want to deliver.

Most of healthcare is delivered locally, in ambulatory practices of small groups of doctors, staff, and patients and the technology that connects them. In Dr. Paul Batalden and Marjorie Godfrey's terms, it is a microsystem of care.

We assert that the patient-doctor relationship still counts as the highest priority in the mind of the person seeking care. We have heard it suggested that certain groups of people—millennials, Gen X, or whatever category you lump people into—care only about the technology. We think people are misguided in this belief. We do think that younger generations insist on the use of newer and ever-expanding technological advances in prevention, communication, and maintenance of their general health. Yet how it is delivered with technology is an augmentation of the fundamental desire each of us, at any age, has: to be and stay healthy and be cared for. Is it the absence of care and compassion in the healthcare system that makes some people compare and prefer a technology-only solution? If there is no value added or differentiator in the care and service, why would anyone choose a less convenient, more time-consuming and sometimes disappointing process? In the best care, providers use technology to deliver enhanced care to patients in a manner in which the doctor is charged with the responsibility of improving care and pursuing safety for the patient. Technology is an augmentation of the need for a strong link between patients and their doctors.

Too often in the news, in political debates, and in discussions of healthcare, the focus is only on cost, access, and inequities for certain populations. We agree those are important challenges we face. Yet no healthcare delivery discussion should be had without paying attention to the patient's satisfaction with the products and services that are delivered. How good is healthcare, or any business for that matter, that doesn't meet your needs and wants?

We are often at our most vulnerable when we see a doctor, in a position of yielding trust to an authority and, often, sharing our deepest fears, secrets, and hopes. We believe as patients that this person and team of professionals can enhance our lives, well-being, enjoyment, and longevity through their actions. If reducing our patients' suffering, protecting them from harm, is our desire and our goal, shouldn't delivery of an outstanding experience, characterized by courteous care, compassion, respect for the person, and treatment as an individual with unique wants and needs, be paramount?

In many models of care, such as the Institute for Healthcare Improvement (IHI) Triple Aim initiative, patient experience of care is as important as population health and cost. In an earlier project dedicated to improving office-based care, IHI identified *access, interaction, reliability,* and *vitality* as the four key domains of successful delivery of office-based care. If we use a play on words, clearly "AIR Is Vital" in this office-based model and the patient experience, represented by interaction, is a priority.

Where and why has healthcare delivery lost its way in so many settings? Why is *the way* you deliver care not being talked about, emphasized, and prioritized in discussions of healthcare improvement? Is it just assumed? If so, is it assumed it will be delivered in a friendly, courteous manner? Or have patients become so accustomed to poor access, delays in response, unfriendly staff, and brief flyby visits from a doctor maintaining an hourly quota of patients to see, so they don't have time to explore deeper patient needs, that a great patient experience has become a remnant of bygone medical care? (This is revisionist history, perhaps, as there have been longstanding complaints about how healthcare service is delivered.)

It does not have to be that way! Whether you believe health-care is a right or an elective, the truth is that patients should expect better service and demand better care. Patient relationships should be generative, growing deeper and more knowledgeable over time. This belief is not rooted only in good business strategy; rather, it's just the right thing to do. We do believe, however, that providing a great patient experience, along with excellent accessibility and good value for the dollars spent, is a differentiating feature of our care, and thus, good business.

Every process, system, and decision we make is built to enhance the visit and perception of the patient, as judged by them. We want people to know we care. Yet that is not enough in itself. A care team of people—the right people with the right beliefs and heart, plus the best systems of delivery, where intentional friendliness, responsive-ness, and care are built into the delivery—are all necessary compo-nents. The challenge we face to improve the patient experience in all offices is a universal challenge. We should all expect more. It is only by raising our standards that we can start to give and receive more.

LESSON 1
Putting Patients *First*

The manner in which patients choose a doctor is ever changing. They may have high expectations built upon a physician's or friend's recommendation. Or they may have just picked us from a list of names, with no preconceived notion of what to expect or knowledge of who we are and what we can do.

Creating a great first impression is paramount! The time a relationship starts is with the patient's first phone call, email, or text. The tone of the relationship starts from the first contact. From that point on, we are in *building of the relationship* mode. Each phone call, text, email, or personal communication should augment the previous one and enhance the relationship.

If done well, whether the appointment is scheduled online, in person, by social media link, or phone, we have the opportunity to positively shape the patient's experience before they even arrive. From that point on, the experience should only get better.

Does this set us up for failure by raising the expectation? Perhaps. More likely, though, it sets us up for differentiation and is the initial step toward building what we call *loyalists*, not just satisfied patients.

LESSON 2
Answering the Phone Is an Opportunity

Every time the phone rings, we have an opportunity to serve and help. The person on the other line has chosen us over many other practices. We're in the business of helping patients and convincing them that we are the best place to protect, correct, and enhance their eye health and vision. A ringing phone means that you're getting the word out about your practice, and talking with each caller gives you a chance to further enhance your image.

> We're in the business of helping patients and convincing them that we are the best place to protect, correct, and enhance their eye health and vision.

Salesman and author Zig Ziglar[2] used to advise that the phone ringing is really opportunity ringing, and he was right.

---

2   Zig Ziglar, *See You at the Top* (Gretna, Louisiana: Pelican Publishing Company, 2000).

LESSON 3
Smile When You Say That

Many studies have shown that callers can usually recognize when the person answering the phone is smiling. The reason? The enthusiasm and clarity of your voice improves when you smile. If patients recognize that you are smiling, you might just get a few smiles in return from them. We have heard people recommend putting a mirror next to each of the phones or using some other symbol to remind staff about this. We have a simpler solution. Expect it— demand it—of anybody and everybody who represents your office on the phone.

Whenever we call in to the office, we are listening for how a staff member answers the phone and greets us. If it is friendly, clear, and welcoming, we'll compliment them on the spot—immediate reinforcement of a positive behavior. Compliment your staff when they do it, and correct them when they don't.

Answering the phone well is something that should be expected of each person on staff, even doctors! Answering the phone with a smile and enthusiasm is part of the way we demonstrate friendliness and build good relationships from the beginning.

LESSON 4
Greet Everyone with a Smile and Make Eye Contact

Of the moments of truth (thanks, Jan Carlzon) in patient care, the most important for setting the tone of the visit for patients is the initial greeting as they walk in the door.

It is the responsibility of every staff member within view to do the following:

- Make eye contact

- Smile

- Say hello

Making eye contact and greeting every patient who arrives in your office with a smile and a hello seems so basic—isn't that the way you want to be greeted whenever you arrive anyplace new? The days of your patients having to ring a bell, knock on a glass window (worst of all smoked glass), cough, or sneeze to get your front office staff's attention are over. It was inconsiderate before, and it still is. When the door opens, all eyes and attention should be on the person entering.

And if you want to take it up a notch, greet them *by name*. Some of our very best receptionists and staff are experts at recognizing people by name just as they walk in the door. Some people have a natural talent and ability for doing this. Other people excel by looking ahead at the schedule. Who we expect to see is right in front of us on that schedule, right? Let's say that a new patient, Mrs. Barker, scheduled herself along with her two children for exams at 9:00. Guess what—the lady who enters at 8:58 with two kiddos, one with a teddy bear and sippy cup and the other in a Titans T-shirt, is likely Mrs. Barker. Greet her by name: "Hi, Mrs. Barker. We've been expecting you. Welcome to Cool Springs EyeCare. And these must be Jamie and Adolphus! Hi there, kids—we're glad to see you too."

It's also good practice to smile and say hello every time you pass someone in the hall. If it's a patient you know, say, "Hi, Mrs. Henson." If it's someone you don't know, pause briefly and say hello anyway. If you're so inclined, compliment them on something—their smile, their clothing color choice, their hairstyle, or whatever. We encourage our staff to compliment patients.

The same thing applies to a staff-member-to-staff or staff-to-doctor encounter. Staff members need to know you care, and they appreciate a friendly greeting or compliment just as much as your patients. Friendliness is contagious. It starts with and is perpetuated by each and every one of us in the office.

LESSON 5
Welcome to the Office!

Publicly display a welcome list for your new patients in the reception room. Make sure you let those new patients know from the very beginning that you know they're there and are glad to have them.

What about HIPAA? Remember, HIPAA does not imply you can't recognize a patient by name. It does require that no medical diagnosis or patient health information be announced. We would *never* say, "Welcome, Mrs. Jones, for your cataract check today!"

Patients want a personal relationship, to be known, recognized, and feel special. Welcoming them in this way helps to do just that. Have you ever been welcomed this way in any other office? Yeah, we didn't think so. We like the differentiation it provides.

While you're at it, welcome everyone coming into the office that day. Having a meeting with an industry representative or an area banker? Whoever it is, welcoming them this way will often amaze them. They'll be delighted they were recognized and singled out. This starts business or vendor partner meetings off on the right note.

Of course, this requires preparation and communication. We all need to be *aware* of who's coming in, and someone needs to be responsible for telling the person in charge of putting up the notices who is coming.

LESSON 6
It's a *Reception* Area

You know that big room out in front of your office? If your intention is to make patients wait, call it a *waiting room*. However, if your intention is to greet and make people comfortable while taking care of their eye problems, call it a *reception room*. Fine anybody on staff—$1 for any staff member and $5 for any doctor—each time they mess up and call that room by the big *W* word. Put all the money you gain from this into a fund and take the entire staff out to eat. (I've even seen people go to a buffet where there are no servers for this dinner. Get it? A "no waiting" party.)

We know this sounds corny, but use whatever it takes to eliminate the mentality that waiting is a normal part of a doctor's office visit. Like the bells at the reception desk, the wood-grain signs, and the doctors who mumble and don't explain why and what they're recommending to patients, those mindsets should have been exorcised from medical practices long ago.

LESSON 7
You Do a Lot—Make Sure Your Patients Know It

Patients need an introduction to the services we provide. You got 'em excited with the introductory contact, and they have an impression about the experience they are about to have. They were greeted with a smile and friendly person at the front desk and liked the ambience, friendliness, surrounding decor, and customized information about their wants. Now it's time to make sure they know all of what you do. Here is an excerpt of an in-office, tablet-led video tour (it could also be a brief personal introductory tour), introducing patients to our range of available services.

Welcome to Cool Springs EyeCare!

Welcome! We are particularly glad to have you as a new patient. We are going to get started with your comprehensive eye health and vision exam in just a moment; however, we think it is important for you to know a little bit about some of the services we offer here at Cool Springs EyeCare.

But first, how did you hear about us, and what made you choose us? Google searches, office location, and insurance plans do bring in some patients, but our number one source of new patient referrals is our established patients! We hope after today's visit you'll be sending your friends too!

You have started in our reception room. (By the way, we never call it a waiting room, as we never intentionally want to make you wait.) We work hard at being both personalized and efficient.

In our optical department, you may have noticed a wide array of frames. Not only will you see our displayed frames, which come in many price ranges, but we also have a virtual inventory of tens of thousands of frame styles and colors. Don't see exactly what you want? No problem; we can likely get it.

We provide comprehensive eye health and vision care at each of our offices. Our doctors are very experienced and fit a wide variety of soft, astigmatism, continuous wear, and bifocal contact lenses.

Our doctors have been involved in corrective eye surgery from the early evolution in the 1980s through the advanced custom LASIK and implantable contact lenses of today. We have a surgeon on staff for LASIK, cataract, and other surgical needs you may have.

During your examination today, we will be performing a number of important tests. They help us determine your refractive state (your prescription), your muscle balance, and your eye health.

To perform the best examination, we invest in state-of-the-art equipment. From the Optomap, which allows us to evaluate the peripheral part of your retina without dilation, to advanced side vision and glaucoma testing devices, we seldom have to refer you elsewhere for any tests.

We see all ages of patients—and we do mean all ages! We start with our InfantSEE program, which is a free eye exam for infants from birth to one year of age. From birth to one hundred years plus, we can and do take care of you.

Here are a few specialties offered that may benefit you or your family:

Dry eye specialty clinic: Gritty, scratchy, watery, or irritated eyes are common in Middle Tennessee, especially with all the digital devices we use. This clinic specializes in treating ocular surface disorders, the most common problematic eye diagnosis in America.

Sports vision is an area of particular interest to our doctors and to many of our patients. Eighty percent of what we process in athletics comes through the eyes. We can help improve recognition, reaction, and response time as well as accuracy in any sport you play.

Reading difficulties and attention problems are often the result of eye muscle, visual processing, and function problems. Feel like you or your child has a tougher time reading and comprehending than others? Our doctors in Performance Vision Therapy can make life-changing and long-lasting improvements to learning and confidence.

Forty percent of children develop nearsightedness, and it's an even higher percentage if one of the parents is nearsighted. We can slow the progression of nearsightedness in our myopia (nearsighted) control specialty.

The number one persistent side effect of traumatic brain injury (TBI) is poor convergence. Difficulty reading or feeling disoriented or "not right" are normal post-TBI. Our fastest-growing specialty, TBI therapy, assists patients—those who have had a concussion, stroke, or other neurologic disorder or those with posttraumatic stress disorder, Parkinson's, or multiple sclerosis—to function in the home and outside world more normally.

Cataract surgery is the most commonly performed eye surgery in America. Get all preoperative, postoperative, and surgery here in our office, with convenient ophthalmologist surgical care, through our surgical services specialty.

Educating patients and providing a healthcare experience that is doctor-patient-relationship driven—that's what we are all about. The Tiger Institute for Cooperative Learning teaches eye doctors, other doctors, leaders, administrators, and doctor's staff locally and nationally how to raise the level of patient service in their offices.

That's a brief introduction to some of what we do here at Cool Springs. (And you thought we just checked vision and fit contacts and glasses!) That is just one of the reasons we like to say that we strive to offer "more than good eye care … a great healthcare experience!"

After your exam, we are always accessible to you. You can call us, reach our doctors twenty-four hours a day for emergencies, or take advantage of our web-based care.

We are ready to start your examination pretesting now and get you ready for the doctor. Grade us in any surveys you may get. We really do listen, and many of the best things we do and you'll experience came from patient suggestions.

We really appreciate you choosing us and are glad to have you as a patient in this practice. We hope to care for your and your family's eyes for a long time!

LESSON 8
Greeting the Patient IN the Reception Room

Don't you hate it when a nurse, medical assistant, or technician comes to the interface between the reception room and the back office clinical areas, yells the patient's name, and then looks around to see if anyone stands up?

Our nurses, technicians, or doctors greet a patient personally *in* the reception room and introduce themselves, always using the patient's name and their own name. "Hi, Mrs. Jones. I'm Jane."

We also introduce ourselves to anyone accompanying the patient. It may be a spouse, parent, or child. The accompanying person's name should be recorded in the medical record in a manner such as, "Accompanied by son, Jose, today."

We follow up with what's going to happen next. "I'm going to do some preliminary tests and get you ready to see Dr. Kegarise." Using the doctor's name here reinforces the patient-doctor relationship and staff-doctor teamwork. Further, it verifies the doctor the patient will be seeing, which is important in a multidoctor practice.

It is a hard habit to break for some people, as the yell from the door is so endemic in healthcare culture. But this habit can easily be broken if the person doing the handoff from the reception desk identifies the clothes the patient is wearing. And it's even better if the person greeting remembers the patient from their last visit. This is an example of strategy leading to operations. If we want to cement ourselves in patients' minds as a relationship-based, service-driven practice, then service behaviors must be woven into our daily processes.

LESSON 9
Help Me Up So I Don't Go Down

We have a passion to help prevent falls. We train our staff to assist patients who have trouble walking. We instruct them to stand by the patient and extend a bent arm that can be used as a brace for the patient to stabilize on. We don't pull the patient up; we let them use that arm to pull themselves up.

Despite our training in this procedure, we allow too many older patients who are noticeably frail, who often have a cane or walker, to rise on their own. Training and knowledge are only good if they are being implemented and demonstrated consistently. The time patients need us most is when they rise from the exam chair and take their first step, not after they have already risen

> Training and knowledge are only good if they are being implemented and demonstrated consistently.

and started walking. (Of course, we should help them then too, if needed). But let's first make sure we *never* have an unexpected fall when a person is getting up out of a chair. By staying close to the chair to assist a rising patient, we can more easily catch them if they fall or break their fall to minimize potential injury.

The morbidity and mortality rates associated with falls and broken bones, particularly hips, in the elderly are very high. We must all do our part to make sure it doesn't happen in our offices when patients are under our care.

LESSON 10
Have Someone in Charge of Care

If you really want to give personalized care, try not to shuffle one patient between seven different people. Or if you must, at least make sure that patient knows who is *primarily* in charge of their care for that day. How do you do this? One way to do this is to have the technician who initiates the examination process, dilates the patient's eyes, or scribes for the doctor hand the patient her own business card. We like them to say, "Mrs. Jones, just to remind you, I'm Amy. You'll be seeing Dr. Johnson today, but I am in charge of your care. If there's anything I can get you or if I can answer questions, today or any time after you leave the office, I want you to contact me personally. My number's right there on the card."

Think of the number of patients that you see. If every one of those patients has one of your practice business cards, whether it's a doctor's or a staff member's, don't you think that a few of those patients are going to share that with some of their friends? More importantly, isn't this the type of care and personalized service connection you would want at a doctor's office?

LESSON 11
Wait, Don't Walk So Far and So Fast

When walking with a patient, do just that—walk *with* them. We see this mistake all too often. A scribe leaves the room intending to lead the patient to the optical department or checkout, and the next thing we see is the scribe five steps ahead of the patient! We see the patient turning their head left and right, wondering where their help went.

After helping the patient up from their chair (if needed), walk with them, and if you lead them, don't get more than a step and a half ahead. You should be able to reach out and touch them. Any farther and you are not walking *with* them. Dialogue should be going on during a walk with the patient (also when greeting a patient in the reception room and taking them to the exam room). That communication best takes place when you are in touch (literally and figuratively) with your patient.[3]

---

3   Unless we are maintaining community-based social distancing, at which time certain modifications for safety must be followed.

LESSON 12
A Conjunctivitis Did Not Just Walk in the Door

We have treated a lot of patients with eye maladies over our careers.

We have seen these patients walk in distressed and leave with treatment and reassurance.

We have never seen a diseased eye walk in.

No keratitis knocks at the front door. No glaucoma checks in at the front desk. And no conjunctivitis sits down in my exam chair.

People do, though, and these people may *possess a diagnosis*—but they are *not a complaint or disease.*

We've heard it all too frequently in other clinics and in other settings. "Doctor, we have a foreign body in room one, an abrasion in room two, and an optic neuritis just checked in up front."

Really?

Practice this in your office and correct anyone who stumbles and forgets: "I have a *patient* with a foreign body in room one; there is a *man* in room two with an abrasion; the *lady* presenting in room three has optic neuritis."

We correct, protect, and enhance eye health and vision. But we only *treat* patients and their conditions. A condition will never present itself—it's always a patient.

LESSON 13
I Can Hear You—Why Aren't You Taking Care of Me?

We encourage keeping a constant focus on our patients. We also embrace a fun, collegial, and good-natured kidding esprit de corps among our team. Balancing both is critically important. But when staff are talking near or outside a patient exam room, it better not break HIPAA rules, and it better be clinically focused.

Imagine you are sitting in an exam room, waiting for the doctor to see you. You want good care, but you also have a busy schedule. You've started to consider how much longer this visit will take. Will you have time to look at new frames? How many people are in front of you to be seen? Those are the things that do fill idle time in people's minds when they are waiting.

Now if you are that patient and you hear people cutting up or laughing out in the hall or near the door, do you think, "Wow, must be a great place to work. All those people have fun and get along?" NO! What you think is, "I'm waiting and those people are playing around. They must not care about me!"

Take care not to have personal discussions overheard by patients waiting. No loud talk. No loud laughing. The focus should be on the patient.

LESSON 14
Personal Info Is as Important as Medical Info

In a relationship-focused business of any type, including healthcare, each of the systems in the office should be designed to enhance the relationship. For more understanding of the importance of this, read *The Discipline of Market Leaders* by Fred Wiersema and Michael Treacy, which is on our recommended books list in the appendix.

Doctors, assistants, techs—everybody in the office—should capture and record any valuable bits of personal information they learn about a patient and put it in their record. Scribes, do you think the patient and doctors are just talking football? Nope, we're enhancing our relationships with patients, and you better be recording it. Here are some examples of information we've captured about patients:

- Oregon State football fan

- played baseball at Kansas

- went to Texas Tech and majored in accounting

- second home on Lake Ford

- caring for mom with Alzheimer's

- three kids and moved one year ago from North Carolina

- talked with JLK about hot chicken places

- loves bourbon

- going back to grad school at Vanderbilt

- wrote a book on relationships

- Dr. Keg kidded about being a Michigan fan

- collects old Ford Shelbys

- wife is sick with breast cancer

- traveling to Italy summer 2020

You get the idea. This year's conversations are the start of next years' discussions—or whenever the patient is seen next.

LESSON 15
Shhh—Use Soft-Touch Keyboards

When scribing, the technician or assistant is like a courtroom stenographer and should attempt to catch all of the conversation—if someone is talking, the scribe ought to be typing! The scribe should document the essence of the doctor's conversations with the patient and be as nondistracting as possible (until getting the handoff from the doctor—but that's a separate technique).

So please, scribes, don't ask questions of the doctor or do anything while the doctor is engaged with the patient. We value and want to elevate the importance of the patient-doctor relationship in our care. And you should always use soft-touch, quiet keyboards.

LESSON 16
Duck! And Don't Slam the Door

When a doctor and scribe are in an exam room with a patient, we make every attempt to not open the door until we are finished and the patient is leaving. Once in a while, though, it is unavoidable. Another staff member may want to get an urgent message to the doctor, or the last patient has a question that only the technician in the room can answer. In those cases, it is important that the scribe is as unobtrusive as possible.

If you have to leave the room, duck down to avoid obstructing the patient's view of the eye chart. On the way out or back in, don't slam the door! Open and close gently to cause as little distraction to the patient as possible. The patient is paying for the time with the doctor. Everything we do should be focused on the patient, their needs, and their care. Anything else, such as a technician walking in and out repeatedly or a door being closed too loudly, distracts from the care and experience.

LESSON 17
Education Is a Part of Care

Our doctors and scribes are really good at educating and explaining to patients about their diagnoses, treatment options, doctor recommendations, and prescriptions. That said, we don't want education to be optional. We want it to be a part of the visit.

Here is an example of what we *think* we say as doctors and what we *intend* the patient to hear:

Doctor: Mrs. Jones, today I found that your prescription does need to change as you are more nearsighted. You also have blepharitis, which is an inflammation of the eyelids. I am going to prescribe some medicated pads for that. I'm watching you for glaucoma due to your family history and what I see at your nerve, so we'll be having you back for some testing."

Yet here is what the patient *actually* hears and remembers:

Patient: Mrs. Jones, nearsighted … eyelids … prescription … testing … come back.

Because of the disparity in what we want patients to know and what patients can likely absorb, we reinforce what we say. First, as one of our moments of truth, we add the reiteration of findings as a step in patient flow. This is the scribe summarizing the bullet points again for the patient, either after the doctor hands off authority at the end of the exam or at a designated area after leaving the exam room. Second, we customize our own handouts and summarize what the doctor has said in writing.

In the case above, the handouts given might be on the following:

- nearsightedness

- blepharitis

- lid scrubs

- glaucoma suspect testing

In this manner, we are emphasizing the important points in three different ways: via doctor discussion, assistant reiteration of findings, and written educational handouts. Of course, patients can also call, email, or text us with questions, but the patient educational handouts also serve as a professional business card, reminding patients of their eye doctor and our findings. It is not uncommon to hear someone say, "I came across that handout you gave me, and it reminded me that I needed to come in—and I made an appointment for my husband too."

It's another reminder of "no sinner was ever saved with one sermon." (See lesson 94.) Find multiple ways to help patients understand and remember their diagnoses and the reasons for their treatment plans.

LESSON 18
Certainty Is More Valued Than Uncertainty

Every contact lens and glasses order should end with a promise date, such as, "Your contacts will be at your door in four business days" or "Your glasses will be ready to pick up in eight days. That would be Wednesday, October 25."

> We want to make a pledge to patients. It's how they build trust in us.

There are two vitally important concepts illustrated by these examples:

1. We are making a promise to the patient. Great service organizations do this. We want to make a pledge to patients. It's how they build trust in us. It also gives the patient the chance to counter with something like, "Oh, I was going out of town on that Wednesday. I really wanted my glasses before then. Any way to get them here on Tuesday?" If we hadn't promised a date, we would never have known about the patient's Wednesday trip. We would have thought we were providing great service, when in fact, the patient had a different expectation. And of course, it's the patient's expectation that counts the most. Promises like the optical or contact lens delivery date force conversations. Most of the time they meet the patient's needs; sometimes (we hope) they exceed their expectations! If the promise doesn't meet their expectations, it gives us a chance to be heroic! Let's see if we *can* get those delivered in three days instead of four. Then the optician owns it and is responsible for communicating with the patient, even after the visit. The "hot board"

(see lesson 71, "It's Getting Hot in Here") we use keeps us all aware of our patients' special needs, so any of us can contribute to meeting or exceeding expectations. When we do achieve that superior level of service, each employee gets a little more feeling of "we," and the culture of *this is just what we do* is embraced and evident to all.

If we can't do it, then we have to communicate *that* (see lesson 19, "And I Would Do Anything for You, But I Can't Do That"). For example, "How long will you be gone? Maybe I can send the glasses to your hotel in Tallahassee?" Another chance to be heroic and get a WOW! (More on WOWs later.)

2. Making a pledge to patients requires a two-sided business understanding—not only what my patient needs but what my lab can and should do. Companies talk about wanting to be our "partner." Just lip service, in my opinion, unless we tell them our expectations and they say, "We *can* meet those standards." If we promised four, eight, or twelve days to the patient, then we are really expecting a three-, six-, or ten-day delivery cycle time from order placed to order received (by us). True partnerships are built on setting, monitoring, and achieving agreed-upon supplier standards.

Patients are rewarded with better care and service. Labs that can reliably meet the standards are (or should be) rewarded with more business. Our patients want predictability and for us to keep our promises. Our suppliers must help us with this, and to the extent that they do and we each meet each other's expectations, our partnership will develop and grow. In our supplier standards for optical (see chart below), we track and expect timeliness (four-eight-twelve/three-six-ten), service, cost, and quality (less than one in one hundred rejected) goals to be achieved. Achievement of these targets helps patients, helps our supplier partner labs, and helps us to differentiate as a business.

SUPPLIER STANDARDS

Supply: <u>Optical Laboratories</u>

Department: (circle one)

Administrative   Contact Lens   Optical   Surgical

Date: _____

Key Person: <u>Optician 1 and 2</u>

FEATURE	VENDOR 1	VENDOR 2	VENDOR 3	EXPECTATION
Quality	8	9	8	<1/100 rejected
Turnaround Time	10	7	8	3-6-10
Cost	8	8	10	Comparison
Service	9	10	10	*See List
Overall Rating	8.75	8.5	9	
Percent Business	60	30	10	

Comments:

RATING SCALE:

10	Outstanding—far exceeds standard or new level
7–8	Above average relative to standard
5	Meets standard
2–3	Less than standard
1	Fails to meet standard

VENDOR/SUPPLIER	CONTACT PERSON/ TITLE	PHONE NUMBER
Riverview		
Bestest Labs		
Cold Springs EyeCare Lab		

LESSON 19
And I Would Do Anything for You, But I Can't Do That

While the singer Meat Loaf would do nearly anything for love, even he had his limits. So do we, and so do you. There are situations that occur in patient care where we just cannot fulfill the patient's request. Perhaps it is an outrageous request. More likely, even with creative thinking, we just cannot figure out a way to satisfy the patient need.

We believe great service and hospitality relationships are not built on always saying yes. In fact, it is very important to be able to say no. The key is to be able to say no in an honest, forthright manner, yet always follow it with what you *can* do. With accelerated benchmarking, we learned this as one of the principles of service at Fairmont Hotels (see lesson 62, "Accelerated Benchmarking—Disney-esque Hierarchy").

Our philosophy is that it is completely okay for you as a patient to ask. And it is also completely okay for us to say, No, we can't do that, yet we can do this. This minimizes angering patients who think you or your staff are just not trying to help them. It also makes staff feel more comfortable and empowered to come up with their own solution or alternative.

Here are some examples where the patient wants something we can't or shouldn't do, yet our staff creates an alternative that we can fulfill:

Patient: I would like my sunglasses with my prescription filled in thirty minutes.

Staff: I would love to be able to pledge that type of turnaround for you, Mr. Jones, yet due to the large amount of astigmatism, your lens is not in our stock inventory. However, what I could do is get you a soft contact lens to correct your astigmatism and then create a pair of sunglasses for you to go over the contacts. And that we could do in thirty minutes.

Patient: I want to get my full supply of contact lenses tomorrow since I am going out of town the next day.

Staff: Your contact lenses will be delivered in four days. I wish I could get them to you tomorrow, but I can't. What I can do is get you a free box of trials that will last five days, and when your lenses come in, I will personally ship them to your hotel or address of your choice while you are on your trip. Would that work?

Those are just examples. It is good to role-play common or obscure patient requests with the staff and have them come up with alternatives when they are forced to say, "But I can't do that."

Over time it becomes second nature for your team members to follow a "no, I can't" with a "yet here is what I *can* do."

LESSON 20
Change Is Good If You Give It First

More people pay with credit cards now, but there are times at the checkout window when change still needs to be given. Here is how to do it: Always place coins in the patient's hand first. Then give them bills.

Most cashiers do the opposite, putting paper money in the hand first and then coins on top, thus forcing you to carefully balance the sliding coins so as not to drop them on the floor!

Make it easy on patients. It's a small thing, but patients will appreciate it.

LESSON 21
At Y(our) Service

We appreciate and respect our veterans. They sacrifice themselves to provide us freedom and a chance to do what we enjoy and love. For that reason, we always acknowledge veterans by looking them in the eye and saying, "Thank you for your service." We do this for every veteran, every visit. They appreciate it, of course, but it not only affects them. Other patients see us doing this and appreciate that we pay attention to such personal details—and sometimes it encourages them to thank the veteran themselves. It perpetuates an atmosphere of personal appreciation in the office.

LESSON 22
Proud to Be an American

There's too much polarizing and labeling today. We really don't care if you're a Democrat, Republican, liberal, conservative, God-fearing believer, skeptical agnostic, black, yellow, green, blue, white, or red. We all share one thing that ties us together. We are all Americans. Most of us are here permanently, and some are just visiting. Yet we all live in a country that prides itself on the spirit of collective individualism, freedom of speech, and freedom of being. Is this the greatest country in the world? We don't know. Haven't lived in 'em all. But we tend to think it is.

We believe in an even bigger commitment than just that to patients, referring doctors, our staff, and others. We all share a commitment to each other as Americans. And for that, we are both proud and eternally striving to make this country better.

When we purchased our Cool Springs office, we started flying an eyeball logo flag right under the American flag. When we moved—no flagpole. Recently, we decided that, flagpole or not, we'd have an American flag or representation of it proudly displayed in each of our offices.

We hope that when staff and patients see it, we will all be reminded that at the end of the day, we're all Americans, and we're darn proud of that.

P.S. Has anyone ever gotten more mileage out of one song than Lee Greenwood has with "God Bless the U.S.A."?

LESSON 23
I Will Show You to the Bathroom and Back

A great department store in Birmingham, Alabama, called Parisians had a rule for when a customer wanted to go to the bathroom. The employees walked the customer there instead of the usual pointing out *how* to get there. Publix, a supermarket chain well known for service, has a similar practice: if you're looking for something, they will walk you to the aisle where you can find it.

These are fine points of service, and you may say you are not staffed to do this or it takes too much time. How ridiculous. Our businesses are not that big. Yet we do it. It demonstrates a measure of intimacy and attention to the patient or customer to walk them directly to where they want.

We walk patients from the exam room to the bathroom and then wait for them, so we can walk them back to their starting point. Even if it takes my scribe out of the room during care to do so, that is the priority. Courtesy is more important than efficiency. (See lesson 62, "Accelerated Benchmarking—Disney-esque Hierarchy," for more on this.)

Ultimately, it is safer and more private for us and the patient to do it this way. Having a lost patient trying to find the correct exam room after using the bathroom is uncomfortable and frustrating for them and for us. We like to prevent those feelings in our patients (and us), so we go the extra few steps with them.

LESSON 24
Murphy's Law of Clinical Care

Eye doctors know this to be true. It's 4:45 on a Friday afternoon, and the day and week are winding down. That work-in patient (often a referral) turns out to be the most challenging case of the day. Perhaps not for the seriousness but for the potential causes and underlying differential diagnostic options that must be considered.

It is with these patients, during these times, that our integrity as a provider and office shows through. Sure, we'd like to get home and start the weekend early. Sure, we'd like to say, "It's probably this, and the mom shouldn't worry." But you know that's not right. The level of care we desire to provide is not achieved without a level of sacrifice. This is a mom who is worried about her child. She chose us to care for her daughter. Being able to coordinate this care, explain the possibilities, and not come across as rushed or frustrated to the patient or mother—that is the measure of who we are and how we care.

> The level of care we desire to provide is not achieved without a level of sacrifice.

LESSON 25
Double Take

If you're doing any operating room work, have the surgeon's picture taken with the patient immediately after surgery. Give this picture to the patient inside a little card with a nice message, such as, "Enjoy your good vision and this special moment from surgery," and have the surgeon sign it. Patients will probably keep this close at hand—maybe put it up on the refrigerator—and at least show a few of their friends, enhancing the image of your practice. Plus, it's just a nice thing to do!

Think of other internal services where you might use photographs or social media (with permission) to enhance the experience, such as when people get frames or contact lenses:

- "Hey, check out you in your new cool glasses!"

- "Hey, this is how you look without glasses."

- "LipiFlow: treatment for the better eyes you deserve."

You get the *picture*!

LESSON 26
Doctors Should Make House Calls

After a surgery, we recommend that our operating surgeon call the patient personally at home to make sure everything is going well. This makes such a positive impression on patients and their families. You can't underestimate the power of this sincere, extra level of concern. Fortunately for us, very few ophthalmic surgeons in other practices do this. Their ego tells them that fifteen minutes of their time to make these phone calls is not a worthwhile investment. We want to personally thank them for adopting this attitude, because their inability to look at eye care from the patient's perspective is great for building our business and differentiating us!

LESSON 27
Honesty Is the Best Policy

Despite our can-do positive approach to responding to our customers' needs, we believe it's important not to overcommit. If you can accomplish a task, tell the person you can and expect them to hold you to it. If you can't accomplish the task, admit to it at the time, and perhaps you can revisit it later. If you are not sure what you can do, be honest with the patient and outline the obstacles to getting it done.

By being honest with patients, you may find they change the parameters of their demand, modify their requirements, or change the time frame. We still believe that honesty is valued in business relationships and society in general. In fact, being honest is the first of our beliefs and behaviors (see lesson 38, "We Believe in BBs"). If people learn that they can trust what you tell them and that you are being a straight shooter, in the long run, you and the practice win—even if the answer you give them on a given day is not what they had hoped for. Building trust and credibility on a long-term basis is what good customer relationships are all about.

LESSON 28
Provide Charitable Care—Internally

We ought to be a resource of information to our patients regarding their options for obtaining supplemental and charitable care. It's the right thing to do. It makes you feel good in the heart, and, with rare exceptions, the patients you decide to provide for in this manner are very deserving.

We designate someone on staff to have knowledge of this area—or, even better, provide a listing of all the available companies, vendors, and agencies that can provide help with meeting care needs. We have found that patients who are truly willing and deserving will help you locate support rather than expect you to provide it all. Make sure you know who provides the support, how much support they provide, how one qualifies to get it, and how long it takes to obtain the assistance. This is one way we demonstrate our connection to the community as a patient advocate.

LESSON 29
New Patient Cards and Personalized Notes

It is our goal to say thank you to every new patient. To do so, we have a standard logo note card, and the scribe or doctor jots a handwritten thank-you note to the patient. It can be brief and personalized, such as, "Mr. Smith, it was great to meet you today and see you for your eye health exam. Thanks for choosing us. I am confident that the change in your glasses will really make driving easier at night. See you next year, Dr. Jacobs." Inserting a business card is a good idea too.

In this way, we add to the personalization of our service. As our former community relations director Jodi Strock used to ask us, "Who gets personal notes from their doctor? No one!" It really sets us apart.

We also encourage notes on other subjects, which may be as simple as these: "Sorry about the loss of your pet," or "Really enjoyed talking to you about your Israel vacation. What a fantastic trip!" And don't be afraid of a little humor: "To all my Wolverine patients … go, Buckeyes!"

Extra notes enhance the doctor-patient bond and show patients we care about *them* first and *then* their eyes.

LESSON 30
Even If You Leave, You Are Always Welcome Here

Patients leave for many reasons. They move out of town. They move to another part of town and are far enough away that it becomes logistically difficult to continue. They want a second opinion. They hear from a friend about that friend's eye doctor and want to try the doctor. They get mad or frustrated. They just aren't embraced into our culture enough to feel a sense of mutual connection. They don't want the connection, service, and generative relationship and look at healthcare as more transactional, seeking the cheapest place to get what they want. In all cases, we will help them with a transfer of records, according to well-established healthcare guidelines and HIPAA laws governing such communication.

There are a few extra things we will do, though. First, we will have the most recent doctor who saw them (or their usual doctor) review the chart and records of visits, looking for any diagnoses that may be important to know about. That doctor will then write a note to the patient, telling them that we did indeed approve and forward the medical records and also informing them of testing that they may be due for, conditions for which the next doctor should monitor, and so on.

Why do we take the time to do this for someone who is leaving us? First, because it is the right thing to do. Although it does take extra time, perhaps it helps reduce the chance of a condition being overlooked in the transfer from one practice to another—and that can be sight saving.

Second, it is one more chance to make an impression about the care and concern we have for our patients' vision and eye health. No anger, animosity, or relentless questions about why; just a heads-up:

this is something we have been following and want to make sure it still gets monitored for your vision's sake.

We also tell exiting patients that we will always be there for them. To see them, talk to them, help explain anything they might hear about or want to question, now or in the future. Email, text, letter, or phone, we will be available to them.

If we are unique, as we strive to be, some of these patients will not have as good an experience elsewhere and will return to us for care. It is important for them to know that they are welcome to return—anytime! Many patients have returned and said, "I did not get the service or care over there that I experienced with you, so I'm back, and I will stay." That's usually a patient for life.

LESSON 31
Thanksgiving with Patients

One of the traditions in our office is to close the doors at noon the day before Thanksgiving and invite all staff and doctors to our Cool Springs office for a catered Thanksgiving lunch. We all sit at a long table (many tables, actually!), kick back, and look forward to a nice holiday break. Lunch is usually an hour and a half, and we follow it by decorating the office for the Christmas holidays (trees, wreaths, ornaments, and all of the festive trimmings). That way, when we return on the following Monday, the office is dressed for the season. Typically, we end decorating around 2:30, and then everyone can start their holiday weekend early. This also gives our staff some extra time for travel in the afternoon without having to take a day off work or use their PTO.

We work our service mentality with patients into this festive and fun celebration also. Throughout the year, we keep track of patients who live alone, have no family nearby, have family yet seldom see them, or are just extra special patients for various reasons. We invite those patients to join us for this Thanksgiving meal too.

It is really fun for them to eat and have fellowship with our staff on a more informal basis. We look forward to it, and they do too! We send staff members, who kindly volunteer, to pick up the patients and drive them back home. It is intended to reflect our compassion and care for patients beyond them getting their eye care with us. We think it helps our staff build a deeper connection with patients and demonstrates we really do care more.

LESSON 32
Transferring and Receiving a Call—Rinse and Repeat

We hate hearing our phones ring and not having any idea who it is. Our work phones often don't have the specific caller recognition of cell phones.

We expect that, when transferring a call, our in-house answerer will hand it off well, allowing us to respond appropriately to whoever is on the line. Tell the person you are transferring the call to who is calling, why the person is calling, and what the caller needs, if possible. Then the recipient can be better informed and personalize the way they respond to the caller.

Here's an example of how it should go:

Us: Good morning, Cool Springs EyeCare and Surgical Services. This is Tammy. How can I help you?

Patient: Hi! This is Mary Fourtimes. Dr. Keg wanted an update on the most recent contact lenses he gave me. I wanted to tell him which one I liked best.

Us: Great! Sounds like you know which one you want. In that case, I can transfer you to our tech on call, Sophia. She'll make a note, tell Dr. Jeff, and order the contacts for you.

Patient: Oh, that would be great.

Us: Can you hold for just a minute while I find Sophia?

Patient: No problem.

Us: (Ring over speaker to Sophia.) Hi, Sophia, this is Tammy. I have Mary Fourtimes on the phone. She was trying two lenses at home for Dr. Keg. She knows which one she likes now and is ready to order.

Sophia: Okay, great!

(Call transferred.)

Sophia: Hi, Mary. I understand you found a winner! That's great. Which lens do you prefer?

(Mary tells Sophia which one she wants.)

Sophia: I'll let Dr. Keg know, and he'll be very happy. (Patients like to please their doctors, and we doctors *are* happy to know we've been successful.) Your full annual supply of contacts will arrive at your door in four business days, and there is no charge for shipping.

Good phone handoffs impress patients, lower frustration among staff, and prevent patients having to repeat their needs.

LESSON 33
Smile for the Camera

Capitalize on the predictability of human nature. Nearly everyone likes to look at a picture of themselves. Everyone comments on how poor they look in pictures. Take a featured service you provide and snap an old-school Polaroid of all patients who have that service in your office. (Do they still make Polaroids? Surprisingly, they do.)

> Capitalize on the predictability of human nature.

You'll have to get patients' permission on this one, of course. The nostalgia of having a Polaroid taken will convince a lot of the older patients. Millennials and younger patients have probably never seen such a device (although we have heard that these are coming back in style), so they'll be intrigued by it.

Okay, it doesn't have to be a Polaroid, but pictures should also be a part of a patient's chart. Often the picture in the medical record helps the doctor remember the patient better. Other alternatives, such as iPad or iPhone pictures, can be filed and transferred into the chart. Recently, we picked up a photo printer, which instantly prints two-by-three pictures from an iPhone. We are going to try this! This can provide current technology with the added benefit of a picture you can touch, feel, and post on a service board.

On your photo board, list the patient's name, the date they had service, and which doctor referred them to your office. Publicly display it in your reception area. You'll find that this board becomes a focal point for discussions of services.

LESSON 34
$10-$10-$100 Making Smiles (Yours and Theirs)

One of our charitable givebacks to the community is the 10-10-100 plan. This is something we started with the kids and have extended to the offices. We take a group of volunteer staff members and send them out into the community with $100. The money they receive does not come with strings but rather with instructions. Surprise someone. Reward someone you see who is nice, struggling, or could use a little bit of extra help. We ask them if they want ten $10 bills, five $20 dollar bills, or one $100 bill. It is up to the staff members how many people they want to help and how they want to divide the money.

What we are looking for is not a contribution to an organization. Rather, we want to have them look for and identify someone on a personal basis in our community.

Perhaps they are checking out behind someone in the grocery store line and pay part of their bill.

Perhaps they are eating and see someone sitting alone. They pay their bill.

Maybe they see a child or adult help an elderly person with a task, such as returning their cart at the grocery store, or another normal-yet-polite giving activity. The staff member gives them some money and thanks them for their deed and for making our community a better place.

As much as we want to help the people the staff identifies, we really want our staff members to feel the sense of personal connection and fulfillment to another person, a person who is unsuspecting, surprised, and rewarded by our staff members.

We don't have them say, "This is from Cool Springs EyeCare."

Nope, it's not advertising; it's just money we give to the staff members, so they can give to others personally.

We do have them report back to us in a group follow-up meeting after the Thanksgiving holiday, so we can all share in who they helped, what the people's reactions were, and the feeling it gave that team member. This also helps to give other staff members ideas for the next time we disseminate $10-$10-$100.

The only place we go for our eye care.

Real people helping for real.

After three years, nearly twenty specialists, more than fifteen failed treatment plans, and thousands of dollars spent, this doctor cared enough to really find out what was damaged and needed to be fixed after my daughter had a concussion three years ago.

CHAPTER 2
Focus on Leadership and Strategy

*There are those that look at things the way
they are and ask, Why? I dream of things
that never were and ask, Why not?*

—Robert Kennedy

The most critically important responsibilities in any business are leading the organization, overseeing the strategic process, and setting priorities.

Starting with a vision (especially apropos in an eye doctor's office!) and creating a strongly differentiated impression in the minds of the consumer are building blocks that can lead to success.

A leader's prerogative is to lead and act in concert with the behaviors they seek in their people. Trust can develop when leaders act with integrity and consistency with their expectations of others. Trust is easily eroded though, when doctors and/or leaders play by a different set of rules or say one thing yet do another. Actions do truly speak louder than words.

When a doctor accepts responsibility for the entire care experience of patients, the continuous focus becomes aimed at developing and improving the service processes as well as the clinical process. When a doctor, leader, administrator, or manager limits their focus to only clinical correctness, entropy occurs in the absence of a clear direction. This is when patients notice problems with office attentiveness, responsiveness, and caring. The patient may feel like another number, as if they're being herded through a system of care that is insensitive to their unique human wants, fears, needs, and desires.

When you are greeted warmly at a doctor's office, it could be due to a uniquely outstanding person, yet more likely, it is a great person who has been educated, encouraged, and focused by a leader with a vision to provide an exceptional patient-care experience to every patient.

LESSON 35
Look in the Mirror

Our practice reflects us. The practice values reflect our personal values. The practice mission is a window to our inner soul. What's our mission? If you don't know or can't communicate it, then how are you going to get others to understand it? How are they—or you—going to know when they are performing in concert or conflict with your practice if they don't understand your mission and values?

To say we will manage those instances as they arise is unrealistic. We can't be involved in every phone call and personal conversation or adjust everyone's body language. That would be exhausting, self-defeating—and poor management, anyway. Our best hope is to set a clear vision for the practice and expect all staff to understand it, buy into it, and also help nurture and train others according to that vision.

LESSON 36
The Mission Must Live!

We don't like mission statements—those that do not resonate with patients and staff, that is. And especially those that do not reflect the experience encountered in the business. We try to make our mission live. Live by being visible to patients and staff. Live by reminders at annual reviews, in conference rooms, and during staff meetings. Live by asking doctors and staff, "How are we doing accomplishing our mission?"

The pièce de résistance is when a mission statement is connected to a strategy the practice is pursuing or a staff member's action. Not only do we try to emphasize PIC NICs (see lesson 88, "Have a PIC NIC") when giving feedback but also how an individual person's action reflects our mission and the practice's beliefs and behaviors.

Tying actions to the bigger mission is culturally reinforcing and powerful, if done well, genuinely, and frequently. Success is achieving the connection and alignment between people, strategy, and the behavior we seek.

MISSION STATEMENT

We will protect, correct, and enhance eye health and vision by providing the highest level of care and compassion to patients.

LESSON 37
One Mission, Five Important Goals

The mission speaks to why we exist. Breaking it down further into goals helps our people connect to the whats. In the goals, we remind the team that patient needs will drive our decisions as priority number one.

That priority is accomplished only with a focus on the staff and their growth. Energized and well-trained, service-oriented doctors and staff, acting in concert with the mission, provide better care (period).

In eye care there is confusion and often competition between optometrists and ophthalmologists. It's silly, yet it does exist. Competitive angst and jealousies fly in the face of our mission and principal goal of keeping patient needs as the top priority. One of our career goals has been bringing the two *O* professions together in cooperation for the benefit of patients. Amazing things happen when doctors work together. Respect develops, and patients benefit. Promoting the skills of both *O* doctors is not only what we say, but more importantly, what we do. And patients benefit.

We believe one of the measures of practice success is the extent to which the business is connected to the community. This commitment extends to sharing time, money, and people. It is a goal we have maintained over twenty years, long before "give back" as essential was a thing. The opportunities and needs are greater than our individual business resources, yet we continue to find more ways to fulfill this goal. By doing so, we hope it sets a good example for community-based businesses of all types.

Long ago, we surveyed patients and learned their number one request for a doctor visit was to be treated with respect. We work hard to demand that in the behaviors of our doctors and staff. We have wonderful patients. Occasionally, however, there are patients who seem to think the giving of respect is a one-way street. We believe respect goes both ways, and we won't stand for either party to break this inherent covenant.

The quickest way for us to dismiss a patient from care at our practice (besides sexual, aggressive, profane, or inappropriate personal comments to our staff) is if we find out they are not treating our team with respect. We do expect our staff to bend over backward in their service, respect, and attitude toward patients, even in difficult circumstances or conversations (see lesson 108, "Treat the Person First, Then the Process—Recovery"). Yet if a patient takes advantage of that attitude, we have our staff's back.

Goals add depth to how we accomplish our mission. We again try to remind employees frequently and visibly so goals are remembered. Every year, at a minimum, we receive written feedback from our doctors, leaders, and staff on how we are doing in adhering to these goals.

The goals really support the mission statement by describing what we value in our care and people. Again, making the goals "live" and relatable makes them more understandable and deepens our staff's ability to live and promote our culture.

The goals should guide people in decision-making. For instance, when we have optometry externs or other students, residents, or visiting doctors observing, there may be times when we keep them out of the exam room with a particular patient. Why? Because we know the patient does not want a teaching atmosphere, and patient needs are our top priority.

When someone suggests that it is such a hassle to come in on a Saturday morning and asks why we can't just see more patients during the week instead, we ask how that aligns with making patient needs our top priority.

Having a representation of the Patient of the Week (POW) (see lesson 46, "Pick a Patient of the Week Every Week") in our staff meeting, in a chair that is never sat upon by the staff, is also a reminder that patient needs are our top priority. In fact, we will sometimes reference or mention that during a meeting. "This sounds good to us, yet if Mrs. Jones [the POW] was physically sitting here, what would she say about it? How does it affect her needs?"

We continually connect the goals of the practice to what we do and, often, why we feel strongly about them. This connects our people and starts to shape positive thinking about our goals.

GOALS TO ACHIEVE THE MISSION

1. The patient's needs are our top priority.

2. Our staff environment encourages growth and creativity and rewards contributions.

3. We promote optometry and ophthalmology as a united force in managing eye disorders.

4. We contribute and give back to the community in which we live and practice.

5. We expect all people to treat others with humility and respect, fostering fun, caring relationships.

LESSON 38
We Believe in BBs

Mission accomplished and goals achieved. This can occur only with continual demonstration of the individual behaviors we expect.

We talk about our beliefs and behaviors (BBs) when you start working for us, we remind you during your time with us, we give you your BBs card as a part of your uniform (see lesson 127, "Are You Fully Dressed?"), and yet what is most important is how we reinforce them in our daily management methods.

One of the strongest PIC NICs (see lesson 88, "Have a PIC NIC") we can give is to say, "Jane, we love how you offered a patient a chance for us to personally deliver her contacts, which were delayed. Admitting the reason for the delay and being honest represents our expected BB, *We will be honest*. And that makes us proud. Keep doing that."

Like a strong and visible mission and understandable goals, the BBs are the highest of the priorities. Training for, expecting, and demanding fundamental nonnegotiable beliefs and behaviors is vital to any business accomplishing its potential success.

> Training for, expecting, and demanding fundamental nonnegotiable beliefs and behaviors is vital to any business accomplishing its potential success.

Connecting actions to the BBs helps guide the staff and doctors in how we act in the practice and how we treat patients, vendors, and each other.

We try to give praise to someone by telling them what they did well and how that is so consistent with the BBs we espouse. That is the kind of direct connection that builds culture. Tell me what I did well and why that is so important in the context of how we act every day and what we believe. Powerful stuff if kept alive via managers and leaders reinforcing it.

OUR BELIEFS AND BEHAVIORS

The integrity of our people is our foundation.

1. We will be honest.

2. We will handle all matters of business with integrity and intent to do right.

3. We will admit our mistakes, apologize for one and all, and seek to improve.

We will build close and continuous communication with patients.

4. We will use people's names whenever possible.

5. We intend to build long-term relationships with our patients and families.

6. We will always recommend and provide the best quality and value of products and services.

7. We will make coming here an enjoyable and memorable experience.

Employee involvement and continuous improvement are at our core.

8. We will recognize the great efforts of others.

9. We will create fun and be inspiring.

10. We will continuously strive to improve ourselves, our care, and our business.

When you get down to it, combining mission, goals, and BBs makes a pretty successful framework for how to run a medical practice, business, or country.

IN SUMMARY

US Constitution

- Preamble

- Seven Articles

- Ten Amendments in Bill of Rights and Seventeen Additional Amendments

Our Constitution

- Mission

- Five Goals

- Ten Beliefs and Behaviors

LESSON 39
Strategy Is a Process, Not an Event

When a lot of people hear about strategic planning, their eyes glaze over. The sheer notion that one could predict where you will be *and* what you will be doing in the next year, two years, or even next week is unfathomable.

We do not believe this should be a painful process. Wait! Did I say "process"?

Yes, I did. Our strategic planning is really a process that starts with *input*, which then leads to *goals*, which are then communicated at an annual *out of the office* (yay!) *strategic operational review*. All offices attend, and we have fun, talk strategy, educate, and party! Well, only a little partying. Yet we do have fun and learn together.

We think it is vitally important to have everyone on the team aware of where we were, where we are, and where we are going. Ultimately, each person should feel a connection to the practice goals and have a clear-cut method to fit in and make a difference in their daily activities.

We communicate or deploy the goals and break them down into monthly bite-size nuggets, or *indicators*. These are continuously communicated with progress viewed at the *weekly staff meetings*.

Later in the same year, we think it is important to ask, "How are we doing at achieving those goals?" This happens at another *out of the office* meeting (yay again!) called the *gap review*. Get it? We talk about the goals we set and discuss any *gaps* in our achievement or performance. We believe it is very important to share our progress toward goals with everyone, not at the end of the year but rather while we are in the middle of the process, during the year. There should be no mystery here.

Some people ask, "Aren't you afraid your staff will share that critical practice information with other people outside the office?" Well, we *do* expect professional confidentiality and maintain a *no share* policy. However, we are more concerned with our staff *not* knowing what we are trying to do and how we are doing, rather than with someone outside our office finding out. We are continuously trying to improve, and that demands communication.

More staff meetings are held weekly after the gap review, so everyone continues to monitor our progress. Around September, we start reviewing what has been accomplished and begin to ask and think about what we should accomplish next year. This is captured in a variety of "inputs" from doctors, staff members, lead team members, patients, vendors, and even others outside the organization. Input leads to goal setting at an off-site *owner's review* in October, and those goals are presented to the doctors and leaders to embrace or massage between November and the end of the year. This culminates in another strategic operational review presentation at the beginning of the next year.

You can see that *our strategic plan is really an ongoing process.* It has worked well for us for over two decades, and we continue to try to refine and improve each step. We measure the success by goals being accomplished and variance from planned operational and financial targets.

Is the amount of emphasis on our strategic process worth it? Our historical success suggests yes, as we continue to grow and improve our accuracy in achieving our projections. Most importantly, rather than strategy being a "set goals and hope" event, our process leads to a sense of direction, control, and visible targets for our doctors, managers, and staff to accomplish each year. Here is the process graphically:

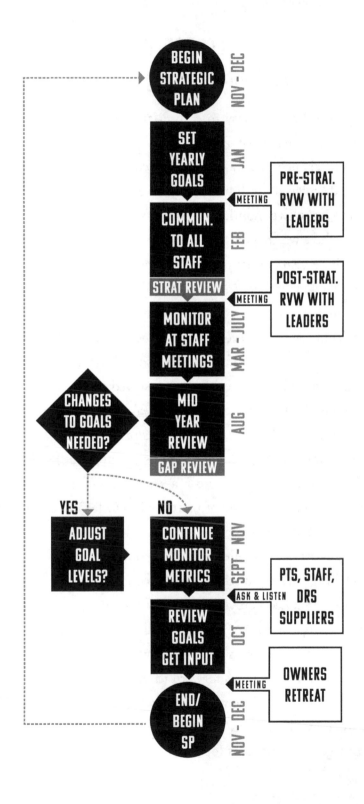

LESSON 40
The Annual Strategic Review

Every year in late February to early March, we close the offices and take all the doctors and staff off site for a strategic operational review. This is our chance to concentrate and communicate on what goals we set and achieved (or didn't) and what goals we hope to accomplish over the next twelve months. Overall, it's a where we were, where we are, and where we are going meeting.

We have held annual strategic review meetings with two doctors and four staff members in an eight-by-eight Days Inn conference room and with hundreds of staff members in a large conference center ballroom—and everything in between. Ideally, the venue should reflect the theme of the meeting. For instance, one year when our theme was "Getting Healthy," we reserved an outdoor lodge with nature trails. That way we could take breaks and long, healthy walks. (We were introducing our new wellness program and set a goal for everyone combined to walk 14 million steps in a year.)

The strategic review is now a combination of presentations: usually a keynote from one of us (usually Dr. Jeff), a celebration of accomplishments, presentation of educational topics, and discussions of key services we offer or hope to offer.

All in all, it's a fun day. We've worn Carnac the Magnificent swami hats, imitated nerdy-researcher types—anything to add a little self-deprecating fun to the meeting. We'll usually plan a dinner or fun activity afterward, so there's time for relaxed and laid-back interaction.

Mostly, everyone looks forward to the strategic review. We'd like to think it's because of the way it underscores and demonstrates how open we are with our staff on goals. Then again, maybe it's because everyone gets to wear jeans for once!

LESSON 41
Laminated Yearly Goal Cards

There is a theme for our care or business stressed during every strategic review. Goals are set and discussed. One of the best ways to keep those goals fresh is to laminate a card (see lesson 122, "Laminate for Emphasis"). This card, which becomes part of the staff's uniform, should reinforce that we each play a part in helping to accomplish the practice's goals. Is it important that you understand your role in the process of us accomplishing those yearly goals? Yes, it is. That connection between job role, performance, and successful accomplishment of goals is for managers and staff to discuss and expect in each area of the practice.

Sharing the goals of the business with the staff via something tangible says these are "our" goals and "I am a part of it" to the staff. As Spencer Johnson and Kenneth Blanchard said in past books, "Don't let someone bowl without showing them the pins." The laminated goal card is but one way we keep the strategic goals set for the year fresh and available for each member of the team. We think of these goals as the pins while we are bowling through the day, week, month, and year.

LESSON 42
Minimize "Staff Infections" by Having Good Staff Meetings

Staphylococcus (staph) is a common bacterium found nearly everywhere on our bodies and in our environment. Most of us tolerate it very well, but sometimes staph infections can be deadly. Hospital staph infections are one of the most pervasive problems for patients and our public health systems. "Staff infections" are also a problem in a practice—those latent staff rumblings of discontent and questions about "Why are we doing this?" or "Why aren't we doing that?" These staff infections can be deadly to a practice.

Below the surface in any workplace are frustrations that occasionally build up and boil over. Most staff infections we see are related to leaders having no true vision of where their practice is going or understanding of what part staff members play in the whole picture. Each person on the team needs to be able to see their piece of the puzzle and how all the pieces interlock.

This doesn't happen passively. It takes a very active communication process. Staff meetings are held on a regular schedule to prioritize and minimize the "I don't know what we're all about or what we're doing" type of feeling. It's the one time in the week when everyone is together and can share information about what's going on in all areas of the practice. We'll tell you our thoughts on *what* should be covered below, but the main goal is to communicate and inform each other about how each of us can share in, contribute to, and help grow the practice and improve patient care.

LESSON 43
Have a Staff Meeting Once a Week, and Always Train

The staff meetings are not casual meetings—like, okay, what do you want to discuss today? They are planned with intention and include discussion of subjects that we feel are most valuable for all of the staff to know, learn about, or review.

Make sure your staff meeting doesn't just become a gripe session. Have each staff member or someone representing each area of the practice give a regular report to all in attendance. Training should be a regular part of staff meetings too. We have staff meeting training every week for about twenty to thirty minutes. The schedule is set up six to twelve months in advance. This can be clinical eye care; optical products; in-office processes; financial management, both personal and practice; critical number trends; or fun times—painting pumpkins for Halloween, writing newborn baby congrats, and so on.

Have a staff summary sheet, which is filled out *in advance*. Identify one person to take notes and type them up. Also, give everyone a notebook to keep all the staff meeting notes together chronologically. For new staff members, the company staff meeting notebook is an excellent training manual to bring them quickly up to speed about what's happening in the practice.

(24 Revenue days)

WOW's, POW's... NOW!

Stories of WOW!!! - Tell us whom you WOW'd or who WOW'd you!

P.O.W.'s

1	7
2	8
3	9
4	10
5	11
6	12

ADMINISTRATOR UPDATE:

Office Manager/Practice Administrator:

	MTD	Monthly Goal	% of Goal
Receipts	$331,000	$450,000	74%

FRONT OFFICE UPDATE:

Front Office Coordinator:

Numbers & Trends:	MTD	Goal	% of Monthly Goal
Total Patients	1110	1,737	64%
Total Exams	568	1042	55%
New Patients	168	347	48%
Dr. Referrals	23	30	77%
Optomap	479	678	84% of exams

Access - 3rd Available Appointment: OD 1:   OD 2:   OD 3:   OD 4:   OD 5:

Practice Access: 0   OD 6:   OD 7:   OD 8:   OD 9:   CL I/R:

Doctor On Call:

front

OPTICAL SALES SUMMARY:

	May 2019 (Goal)	May 2019 (Actual)	% of Goal (Mthly)	Notes:		
A/R	292	238	82%			
Progressives	122	121	99%			
Frames	493	252	51%			
Lenses	592	293	49%			
IOF	120	65	54%			

Trends vs. Goal: MTD   PYM   YTD
Capture Rate   Goal: 55%   Trends: 51%   52%   **49%**

OPTICAL
MANAGER:

SURGICAL UPDATE:

Surgical
Coordinator: Sx This Week: Surgery Next Week:

CLINICAL and CONTACT LENS UPDATE:

          Annual Supply Capture Rate: 41%   Goal: 30%
                              MTD: 35%
TIGER UPDATE:
Coordinator:
                Upcoming Meeting/Courses:
PVT/TBI UPDATE:
Therapist: PVT Patients this week: 32   TBI patients this week: 14

IT UPDATE:

INSURANCE UPDATE:
Insurance Manager:

DOCTORS UPDATE:
OD 1:
OD 2:
OD 3:
OD 4:
OD 5:
OD 6:
OD 7:
OD 8:
Training: Presentor: SUBJECT OF TRAINING

Adjourn, Get ready for WOW moments!!!

"QUOTE OF THE DAY"

---

back

LESSON 44
Staff Meeting Notebooks

Everyone should bring their staff notebooks to the meeting. We often review previously mentioned processes or training, so having the notebook allows for review and demonstrates preparation on behalf of each team member.

We like to personalize each team member's notebook. Our former operations director, Jodi Strock, started this years ago. She would listen to the introduction of the new staff members' likes, dislikes, and personal passions. She'd then reflect some of these passions with pictures on the notebook cover and put "[Staff Member's Name] Staff Meeting Notebook" on the front as well. This was a really nice touch and made it easy to return it to the appropriate person if it was misplaced.

LESSON 45
The Empty Chair Speaks Loudest

At each staff meeting, have an empty chair with a sign on it that represents the POW, or Patient of the Week. (If it's a referral center, we also have a Doctor of the Month.) This represents a tangible reminder that any decision made in the practice affects patients (and/or referring doctors). Ask during the meeting how each of your decisions would affect the POW. If that patient were there, what would they say? What input would they give you about any given decision?

Whenever possible, have a real patient at your staff meeting to listen. You could even consider having them present the training for one of your meetings. This is a great way to drive home the patient-practice connection of your pursuits. There is real power in this. Your guest will appreciate good management when they see it in action.

LESSON 46
Pick a Patient of the Week Every Week

We are privileged to see a lot of appreciative and happy patients. But there always seems to be a few each week who, for one reason or another, stand out and brighten our day. Our staff and doctors vote during the staff meetings on who those POWs are. We send a card that is signed by all of us, congratulating each patient on being a POW. If the patient was a referral, their referring doctor is notified that their patient was selected.

Multiple POWs are fine. It is not the goal to select only one. It *is* the goal to select any and all patients who brightened our day.

When a patient asks, "How did I get this?" we always say, "First, congratulations. Second, you were selected by our whole staff at our weekly staff meeting." We are fortunate to be in a profession where so many people thank us for brightening *their* day with new glasses, contact lenses, or surgery. Yet there are people we see who really brighten *our* day too. So we want to recognize them and say thank you.

We keep each POW on a registry so we can identify, thank, invite, or update them selectively at any time. POWs make a great standing base for a loyalty program.

LESSON 47
Staff Meeting Thank-Yous—Appreciation Notes

Every so often at a staff meeting, we think it is good to take a step back and just say thanks. To each of us, that is. So we put aside the day's training and hand out a card to everyone with instructions to write a personal note to someone (anyone—patient, family, fellow staff member) just thanking them for being there, for providing support, or to give them encouragement. This demonstrates that, although we do care about our staff's work, work is only a part of life.

Reminding your staff to say thank you is a good habit. We each have people in our lives whom we can't thank enough, or don't. This encourages a quiet moment to do that thanking, and, for me, once in a while, that is more important than what we had planned to learn that day.

We don't know to whom people send their personal notes. We don't look. We collect them and send them via the office's postage meter. We care about our people as people first and as great workers and team members second.

LESSON 48
WOWs

At the beginning of every weekly staff meeting, the office manager, after introducing any guests present, says, "Are there any WOWs?" WOWs are a chance each week for peer-to-peer, staff-to-staff recognition and thanks. I'm always encouraged by the sheer number of comments—things like, "I want to thank Mary for covering for me while I went to the dentist." "A WOW for John who retrieved a patient's coat and drove to her house to deliver it." "Our interns deserve a WOW for how quickly they've learned our computer system." "WOW to Dr. Jin, who stayed for a patient running late after hours on Tuesday night."

WOWs are sometimes specific, noticeably heroic efforts, or they can be just a thanks and recognition for someone who does something that is appreciated during the daily routine. There are no rules. The WOWs are not written down ahead of time. They're just spontaneous thank-yous called out in front of the whole staff. We think WOWs speak to our cultural desire to create happy staff as well as happy patients and happy doctors. And this reminder to the staff of that desire is weekly and personal.

LESSON 49
Stick Your Neck Out Award

Every month, or as often as someone wants to do it, we hand out a Stick Your Neck Out Award. In one of our offices, we have a gosh-awful, ugly ceramic giraffe candy dish, complete with a bandage on the neck and a few cracks on the surface. This is the award presented from one staff member to another, who is recognized for going above and beyond in their daily staff-to-staff helpfulness.

This giraffe is proudly displayed on the recipient's desk, and we keep it filled with their favorite candy. (We know this kind of detail about our staff members—*see* lesson 80, "Favorites—We Know What You Like").

We originally got this idea from Dr. Matt Hughes, who incorporated this type of award into his office culture. We have kept it up for seventeen years, and it's just another way for our staff to publicly praise another staff member for doing a great job.

LESSON 50
Crazy Antics Say It's Okay to Do Crazy Good Things

We're not above doing something silly. When we make our monthly bonus, we model the Ohio State football announcer in our staff meeting, saying, "Hands up, fans!" Then one of us runs around the room high-fiving everyone.

One time, when we were rewarding our staff with a nonmonetary yet meaningful "attaboy!" we took them all to learn line dancing at the Wild Horse Saloon and Café in downtown Nashville. How did we announce it? Our fellow optometrist, Dr. Dan Schimmel, and Dr. Jeff suddenly burst into the staff meeting, each galloping around the room on a hobbyhorse and yelling, "We're going to the Wild Horse!" Everyone laughed—some with us, most at us, and they likely remember that entrance more than the line dancing trip!

We're not above doing a Fire Up! (see lesson 51, "Fire Up! Ten, Nine, Eight …") at a surprising time if we sense a lull or less energy at a staff meeting. Doctors are human, too, and need to express their fun side. We believe that adding some fun and being silly, even a little crazy, to get out of the ordinary not only helps staff morale but also emphasizes an important point. To go overboard, outside the lines, in support of a patient may require being a little out of the ordinary. Maybe, just maybe, by our *not* being ordinary at times, we demonstrate to everyone that it's okay—even encouraged—to go above and beyond in your job.

LESSON 51
Fire Up! Ten, Nine, Eight ...

When Dr. Jeff was a Cutco salesman, while sitting in his car in preparation for each sales pitch, he'd energize his mind with a "Fire Up!" What is a Fire Up, you ask?

It's simple. You start with elbows down, fists up at shoulder height (like a boxer in a defensive stance). Then you count down from ten, starting with the left hand thrust skyward; nine with the right hand up, left hand down; eight with the left hand up, right hand down, and so on. You use a slow cadence in your counting that gradually gets louder and louder, faster and faster, until you reach one. Then you follow up with a loud "Boy, do I feel great!"

A little hokey, you say? Perhaps. But psychology and scientific evaluation of moods have proven over and over that posture, attitude, outlook, and energy pay off in positivity and confidence. Even if you don't feel it, you can influence your own psyche by using simple methods such as a Fire Up.

When do we use them in our practice? No, *not* before seeing every patient! But when needed, in department meetings, staff meetings, or anytime we feel like a group of people's energy may be lacking. (Hmmm, this often seems to happen a lot when Dr. Jeff is the speaker.) We're always glad when we call for a Fire Up! It's fun, creates energy, and really does make everyone feel good. Try it yourself or with your team. "C'mon. Ten, nine, eight ... Boy, do I feel GREAT!"

LESSON 52
What We're Afraid Of

Typically, people who visit our staff meetings are captivated by the esprit de corps and rhythm. They say things such as, "Wow, you do this every week? I've never seen such a well-run and fun staff meeting. You can tell that this is a great place to work and you guys really care about your patients."

Occasionally, after seeing the weekly data on the staff meeting sheet, they also add, "You are really open with the practice performance information. Aren't you afraid one of your competitors or someone else outside the office might get this information?"

First, we believe in open-book management.[4] In fact, not just displaying the numbers but helping people understand and evaluate the trends and reasons behind the numbers. We always remind staff or those reporting to the staff that we can see the numbers, but their job is to help everyone understand them. That is the mark of people growing in the organization. Not waiting for the boss to feed them what they should know. Nope, it's right there in black and white. Now they seek to understand why. We particularly look for doctors and team leaders/managers who speak up and ask questions. That engagement speaks volumes to the rest of the team.

> We don't worry about the data falling into improper hands. We're more worried that people on our team might be doing a job and have no understanding of how well they or the practice is doing and why.

---

4   Open-book management as a management construct was written about in *The Great Game of Business* by Jack Stack.

So, philosophically, we don't worry about the data falling into improper hands. We're more worried that people on our team might be doing a job and have no understanding of how well they or the practice is doing and why. Besides, numbers are just numbers. It's a lot harder to create them, understand them, and influence them. That's what leadership is all about.

LESSON 53
Do Not Open the Door—until We're Ready

We have a rule during our staff meetings. We are closed—even if a patient or other person knocks on the door or has a need (obviously, emergency situations are an exception). Some people have questioned this, saying, "You profess to be a service organization, and yet you don't respond when someone is waiting at the door or knocking?" The answer is yes.

Here is our position. We are a service organization, and we do pride ourselves on the service we deliver. But when do you think we reinforce that mentality? In the staff meeting. The dynamics of sitting in a circle and reviewing, talking, and learning together are profound, if they're done well. It's the one hour of the week when we connect and dialogue with each of the people on staff—not patients. They get to hear what the practice owners think is important, and we get to hear what they think and what's on their minds. We all get to see how the practice is performing and in what areas we are struggling and why. That's rich and so valuable—and ultimately makes our patient care better.

The rest of the time, we are in full patient-care and dedication mode. But during our staff meeting, it's full staff care and dedication mode. So we do not open the door during staff meetings. If we do, it is only briefly to try to not disrupt the meeting. Yet it inevitably does—even that little distraction.

Value your staff and the time you have together. Share that time as inviolate.

When the staff meeting is over, we rearrange the chairs and get everyone into their positions. Then and only then do we open the doors to patients—when we are fully ready to be 100 percent dedicated to them.

LESSON 54
The Gap—and I'm Not Talking Jeans

In addition to the input, goals, strategic review, and ongoing review at staff meetings, we hold a gap review six months after the strategic review.

This gap review is kind of a strategic review lite, yet no less important. We close the office for a half to full day to review how well we are doing at achieving the goals from the strategic review. It allows us another opportunity to keep our team engaged in the bigger picture and aware of what we are doing. It also allows us to to see if our efforts are paying off—and why or why not.

The gap review also serves to allow a midcourse correction. If we are not achieving our target goals in a particular area, there is open discussion on what could or needs to change to meet the goals.

The gap review is another all-doctors-and-staff, close-the-office, team-building strategic exercise that serves many purposes. Not the least of which is a chance for the practice owners to be visible and connect with everyone on the team. The staff enjoys this gap review too—it's another day when they get to wear jeans!

The entire staff is cheerful and nice.
They make you feel right at home.

I have never been treated so well in
any place of business.

I love this place!

CHAPTER 3
Focus on Management: Reinforcing the View

Before the beginning of great brilliance,
There must be Chaos
Before a brilliant person begins something great,
They must look foolish in the crowd.

—I Ching

An organization can only grow to the level of its management team's ability. To improve care, once a clear vision, reason for existence, positioning, and differentiation is communicated and emphasized and systems are put in place, you have arrived, right?

Wrong!

The above help you develop a great *approach*, yet *deployed success* that ultimately yields the intended *result* is the goal. This requires management.

It is easy to call someone a manager, but it's much harder to witness management in action. Quality is described by John Guaspari in *I Know It When I See It*,[5] and so it is when observing good management in action. Most healthcare middle managers are promoted after demonstrating good technical skills. It is as if we say, once you master the clinical or technical aspects of your job, you are ready for the next challenge—being a manager. And yet management skills are very different from technical skills. Many managers are ill prepared for the requirements of the job. And it is a particularly hard job. There are competing demands from the boss, doctor, or administrator above and the need to be responsive to those who report to the manager. The amount of expertise and finesse needed to do the job well is significant. Your managers' growth and the management systems built into the office are vitally important to rendering care, building a collegial work environment, and achieving the practice's goals.

Fortunately, the library, bookstore, and internet are replete with theories, methods, and suggested ways to become a better manager. We personally have loved learning from Peter Drucker, Tom Peters, Marc Allen, and companies that have won the Malcolm Baldrige National Quality Award and those managers, leaders, and other successful people who willingly and graciously share their approaches and successes at management conferences and in writing.

Einstein said, "I have no special talents. I am only passionately curious." That describes our management approach, whereby we are a little less interested in the what and more interested in the how and why. We teach our managers to pursue and to learn, using short-cycle plan-do-study-act (PDSA) trials. Managing innovations and having improvements underway, in the queue and envisioned, is a prerequi-

---

5   For more information, read *The Customer Connection* by John Guaspari.

site of managing in an improvement-oriented organization.

We do not try to usurp or replace the teachings of experts on the subject of management, those that have built international reputations with their teachings. We stress a simplified acronym for training managers: StOMPF. This acronym stands for the most important areas or domains that a manager must learn to master. *St* is for "strategic," both in understanding your role in creation of or implementation and tracking of progress toward the business's strategic goals. *O* is for "operations," and that covers areas in health-care such as scheduling and access, patient flow, moments of truth, handoffs, communication with team members, clinical processes and care systems, and all other areas that fall under the operational umbrella of the specialty in which you are involved.

Marketing is represented by the *M*. Often in larger organizations, marketing specialists create the plan, graphics, and collateral materials provided for patients. However, every manager in our organization must be cognizant of their role in marketing a product, service, or cultural mentality in the office. Managers are part of the marketing implementation process team.

The most heavily emphasized, trained, and discussed element of management we spend time on is represented by the *P*: personnel management. This includes how to interview, hire, document, reprimand or redirect, enhance performance, and understand and counsel. These are the behavioral soft skills as well as hard skills in managing people that can't be emphasized enough.

Financial management (*F*) is unfortunately not taught well in our scholastic systems. Very few managers we see at the middle-management level are familiar with the difference between revenue and profit, a balance sheet or an income statement. They may be responsible for budgets in their areas yet seldom receive feedback on where their efforts register successfully (or not) on a profit and loss statement. This knowledge is not above the level of what managers can learn. They, like many others, have not had people take the time to explain the set of financial statements that every business must have and how they can affect those statements positively. We too often see bonus and profit-sharing plans in place in offices, yet the very people who benefit don't have a firm grasp of where those numbers are generated or come from. Knowledge is power, and opening the practice books to the managers is always revealing. Inevitably, they say, "We pay that much for that? From now on I am going to [turn off the lights, clean that myself, keep up with samples, do a more frequent inventory, turn down the heat]."

Additionally, identifying the next person who will rise to the next management level is inherently beneficial. The time to start training managers is not when a crisis of short staffing occurs, but rather, you should be thinking ahead to when and if this person would need to step in.

Continuing to evaluate, identify, groom, train, expose, and teach management skills to managers and potential managers, using an open-book management approach, can accelerate growth in your people, organization, and care. As you elevate these people and their skills, you elevate the care delivered to patients in your office.

LESSON 55
You May Never Know All the Facts, but You Still Have to Make a Decision

Analysis paralysis. It wrecks efficiency by engendering procrastination. Some people are good at gathering facts and data then delegating upward for others to make decisions. If you have been asked to find facts to help support or refute a decision, then do the best you can and leave few stones unturned. That's how you build respect and gain confidence from your team leader or manager. However, when *you* are in the position of needing to make the decision, the responsibility takes on another dimension. With great responsibility for making decisions comes great accountability. For some this is paralyzing. They never think they have enough information or facts to project the best decision, so they don't make one, and things don't get done. Here's how we deal with this.

First, we try to create an atmosphere of creative innovation based on responding to the needs our patients have (even if they might not know they have them). Inherent in that managerial philosophy is throwing spaghetti at the wall and seeing what sticks—which we hope encourages our people to take risks. These are short PDSA cycles that allow for small improvement introduction, tracking of its effect, and decision-making before widespread implementation. Not all good ideas work (we know this for a fact because many of our so-called good ideas have not worked). But some do, and we have had enough successes to encourage innovation and establish a comfort level with failure. No one gets fired for trying, for taking calculated risks. *Dr. Susan and Dr. Jeff* wouldn't be around if we did that!

Second, you can't just substitute your abdominal computer (Dr. Jeff's dad's term) with getting the facts and plotting projections.

Taking the time to analyze and run worst-case, likely, and best-case scenarios is a part of growing as a manager. Reviewing how your projections pan out is how you grow quicker as a leader.

> Don't retreat from that responsibility. Make a stand and recommend or pursue a position. No one expects you to be perfect, but we do expect you to make decisions.

Third, there is a point when a decision needs to be made. Don't retreat from that responsibility. Make a stand and recommend or pursue a position. No one expects you to be perfect, but we do expect you to make decisions.

Clarify in advance whether you are gathering information to make a decision on your own, giving information to others to make a decision, or using some combination of group decision-making. Knowing your part in the process helps you understand your responsibility. If you are charged with making the decision, make it and own it.

LESSON 56
Sometimes the Best Decision Is No Decision

This may sound contrary to what we just insisted on about making decisions. However, sometimes the best decision is no decision— as in, we can't decide yet. Often, when we feel this way, we don't have enough information, or it hasn't been presented in a way that convinces us—yet. This doesn't mean that we *can't* make a decision. It means we haven't *convinced* ourselves to make a decision yet.

LESSON 57
Good Enough to Act

In academic parlance, there is no greater measure of validity than confidence intervals and randomized, prospective, placebo-based clinical trials. Some of the greatest advances we have made in treatment have come through these types of rigorous studies.

In real-world clinical practice, however, innovative organizations are trying to improve across multiple fronts and in multiple areas. There is no time for these types of trials. And if there were, we'd be making only one important advance over a course of years. That pace is unacceptable in a quality-improvement-seeking organization.

Classic innovation theory supports a PDSA cycle for improvements. At any one time, we in our private practice have multiple PDSA cycles going on. As Dr. Don Berwick, former administrator for the Centers for Medicare and Medicaid Services, told me, clinical practice improvements need to be pursued when you have data and information that is "good enough to act."

How does this play out practically? At any given time, we are tracking and gauging improvements in care, service, and flow for patients. This may seem random, but each question yet to be answered is a study for our improvement.

Did the change in the work-up process result in a shorter cycle time for patients today? Did the walk to the car by our staff improve patient satisfaction and delight? Do patients enjoy us serving flavored water to everyone?

The answers to such questions are often gauged via quick evaluations. Not every patient every day of the week, but rather half of one day. If it seemed like it worked, expand to another half day. Never try to gauge too much by evaluating every patient every time. That approach would exhaust everyone and burn the staff out on making improvements.

We track our attempts at improvement on a colored PDSA chart (see the following page). Once we learn from something we try, we share it, both when it doesn't work and when it does. Over time, we have these little projects (the staff thinks it's too often, saying, "Dr. Keg is changing it again!") spelling out better ways to do things, and we integrate them into our regular practice methods.

As much as our practice's service is about the consistent fundamentals, we always stress a balance between consistency and innovation. We call this the managing and balancing *IF*—innovation and fundamentals.

You need to be successful long term, in business processes and in clinical care. We are supportive of evidence-based medicine, and those principles are woven into our clinical protocols for chronic care delivery. But don't hold us accountable for everything needing to pass the standard of a double-blind test. We are eye doctors and have a natural aversion to that term!

Good enough to act is good enough for us.

	PROJECTS IN LIFE CYCLE MO/YR	PLAN	DO	STUDY	ACT	IMPROVE	COMPLETED
1	Your eye care visit and team today cards	▓	▓				
2	Merchandising Optical	▓					
3	New location	▓	▓				
4	Seeds for Seeing Expansion –501C3	▓					
5	Contact lens ordering on site upgrade	▓	▓	▓	▓		
6	New Equip for Mac. Degen.	▓	▓	▓	▓	▓	X
7	New Equip for Headaches	▓	▓	▓	▓	▓	X
8	Innovation – augmented business	▓					
9	Appointment online upgrades (possible)						
10	Glaucoma point project	▓	▓	▓	▓	▓	X
/	Service manual compiled into a book	▓	▓				
/	Expand Premium Appt times	▓	▓	▓	▓	▓	X
	Strategic Plan Packet 2019-20	▓	▓	▓	▓	▓	X
/	New patient Magical Moment tour	▓	▓	▓	▓		
/	Clinical Health coordinator	▓	▓	▓	▓	▓	X
/	"Lids" web based order board in optical	▓					
/	Go Board in Front office (and possible staff area)	▓					
	Hiring guide and short term plan	▓	▓	▓	▓	▓	X
	Optical and contact lens quizzes completed	▓					
/	Enhanced Signage in office for the break/staff area	▓					
/	Expectations for Doctors and Dr. manual	▓					
/	Loyalty Black Eyes and Red Eyes	▓	▓				
	Doctor's as a Unit – compass	▓	▓				

LESSON 58

Think Not What Your Patients Can Do for You but What More You Can Do for Your Patients

Strategic plans tend to focus on gaining new patients, making more money, and/or gaining market share. While generating new patients is an important part of strategy, it is also the most costly. It is better to evaluate what services are wanted, needed, and not being offered to your existing patients and then add them. You have already invested time and money to get them through the door in hopes of building a patient-care relationship. Why not *deepen* that relationship through a multitude of services? Patients will be less likely to migrate elsewhere when they are tied to multiple services that your practice offers.

It is important to not provide a service for which you cannot maintain the same level of consistency or care your customers have come to expect. Whichever services we choose to add, our patients should still expect to be greeted with a smile; a friendly, knowledge-able technician in the workup; a doctor with clear-cut instructions and a friendly demeanor; and well-understood charges and value. You are building relationships. The deeper the relationship, the more trust develops and the more forgiving a patient is likely to be if a service error occurs. By adding additional services, there is a greater chance that an individual patient will recommend one of the multitude of our services to friends. The focus on existing patients and adding services can actually build new patient demand. This results in growth and greater market share at a more reasonable price than marketing efforts.

LESSON 59

Don't Use Cruise Control When You're Driving Downhill—There's a Truck on Your Tail

I've seen it happen way too many times. You have one chief competitor in town. You're constantly jockeying back and forth for the front-runner position. You work exceedingly hard at the start. All of a sudden, your hard work pays off, and you get the upper hand or competitive jump on the competition. At that point, it's time for you to accelerate, to widen the gap between you and your competitor, not keep going at the same pace. Remember the adage by pitcher Satchel Paige, "Don't look back. Something might be gaining on you."

LESSON 60
The Lost World—Laugh at the Scary Parts

We've each had those days. When not only does everything not go as planned, but it goes to hell in a handbasket—and fast. There is an immediate need or problem you are called to deal with at the same time you are already handling something else. Then another crisis occurs, and in your best managerial delegation mode, you say something like, "I'll handle this, you handle that, and Jane will handle the other issue." This is met with "Jane's not here." In situations like this, all you can do is ride it out and do your best. It, too, shall pass.

Our kids were young when the *Jurassic Park* movies came out. Our son, Kevin, really wanted to go, but we knew there were some parts that might be extra scary. So as Kevin and Jeff sat down in the theater, Jeff said, "Kevin, there are going to be some parts that are scary in this movie. If you get scared, just remember it's only a movie, and let's agree to laugh at the scary parts." One time, when Kevin was hiding his eyes and looking away from the screen, Jeff laughed and said, "This is funny; let's just laugh." Laughing at the scary parts got us through *The Lost World*.

If you grab Dr. Jeff in the hall to handle an urgent need and ever see him just laugh, know that he's probably handling two other urgent situations already. He is not laughing at you or the problem. He is just laughing at the scary parts. Sometimes it's the only way to get through them!

LESSON 61
Accelerated Benchmarking—Outside Healthcare

Nearly everyone benchmarks. Understanding and evaluating how similar business competitors do something is beneficial to avoiding the "beat your chest; we do it best" naivety of some managed companies.

We like to take benchmarking to a different and more focused level. We benchmark other organizations, concentrating on a single area in which they excel. Look at the best at what they do best, no matter what their industry.

Here are a few examples of taking a deep dive into observing excellent behaviors in excellent companies, so we can model our similar processes after how they do theirs well:

- How Southwest Airlines turns over gates quicker than its competition.

- How Graniterock, a concrete company, surveys its customers to learn about penetration versus the competition and what influences customer choice.

- How Sewell Cadillac of Dallas reinforces great service delivered with its checkout survey.

- How Discount Tire builds social media communities.

- How Build-a-Bear customizes its customer choices.

- How Cracker Barrel trains new staff and promotes visible employee growth.

There are a hundred-plus (or more) opportunities that exist locally, regionally, or nationally. Find these companies and learn how they do what they do well. Then bring that information back, share it with the leaders and staff, and see if it makes sense to modify, adapt, or improve your similar process. Sometimes you need to go on site, while at other times you can start by reading publicly available resources. Business is filled with opportunities to improve. Why reinvent the wheel when others have already done it well, and you can modify their approach? Quicker, simpler, and more effective, accelerated benchmarking helps you implement positive changes faster and better.

LESSON 62
Accelerated Benchmarking—
Disney-esque Hierarchy

Much has been written about Disney and the creation of a customer experience. We have studied many aspects of its approach. One that is seldom mentioned in healthcare is how it prioritizes.

Frequently, we have to make decisions *not* of right or wrong but rather of *which is* more *right?* Attending the Disney Institute, reading about the company extensively, and personally experiencing Disney led us to a deeper understanding of the beliefs, values, and priorities Disney stresses when training new cast members.

Our accelerated benchmarking was to target Disney on training customer service. An unforeseen benefit was learning that "show" (their word for experience) was not the number one priority. We recognized this parallel with our approach to patient care right away. In any healthcare setting, we must create a safe environment for our patients and staff. Safety is a fundamental underpinning of great service. Thanks to Disney, we use our own version of its hierarchy of service to train all doctors and staff yearly.

It is always fun to hear the responses when we ask, "What is the most important thing we can provide to our patients?" New team members, already embracing the culture, say service, smiles, empathy, politeness—yet the established staff know it is a trick question. The correct answer is safety. This leads to a discussion of what it means to be safe, from the parking lot to the exam room, in the optical and with HIPAA guidelines. A similar discussion is then held on the other three priorities: courteousness, experience, and efficiency.

We use case examples and role-play to emphasize decision-making in the presence of two right options. Although we do aim for efficiency, we do not sacrifice courtesy or elements of patient experience in care. Those priorities are our stakes in the ground. Never speed over safety.

It is one thing to believe. It is better to teach. It is best to provide the framework for good people to make the best decisions when they are confronted with patient-care dilemmas. A hierarchy of priorities in care delivery, learned through our active pursuit of accelerated benchmarking—and visiting Mickey!

K2 Practices Hierarchy of Service Delivery

4. EFFICIENCY

3. EXPERIENCE

2. COURTEOUS

1. SAFETY

LESSON 63
Never Apologize for Fees

A lot of thought goes into setting our fees. Whether it's for optical services, contact lenses, professional services, or products, part of running a good medical office and business is pricing things. Pricing should reflect and be consistent with your business strategy.

Low-price, budget, discounted approach? Set fees lower, promote discounts and twofers, lower the prices of your products. With that approach, pricing is consistent, and money is made more on inventory turn than on profit margins.

High value–added service and relationship approach? Fees need to reflect the extra staff time, expertise, and energies needed to develop this differentiation. Sure, you want a good product turnover, but you are more likely to make more of your money on profit margin.

Here are some rules we go by:

- Price consistent with your strategic positioning.

- Evaluate pricing as a regular part of the business financial operations.

- Never apologize for your fees. If set well, you're worth it.

- Remember who decides if it is a good value: the patient or customer.

LESSON 64
Name's on the Door!

In the *Boston Legal* TV show about a law firm, William Shatner, an attorney with the firm, frequently said when wanting to get his way, "Name's on the door." This, of course, meant no discussion, I'm a partner, and therefore, my decision stands.

We have a very open-book management culture in our office (thanks, Jack Stack!), and for the most part, that's good. Often, we'll listen to dissent and contrasting opinions even more or longer than we should. While doing so, we learn how well thought out, researched, and factually based a person's opinion may be. Sometimes it changes our mind. When the opinions are well constructed, they always impress us and build increased respect for the person. And respect leads to trust.

We don't do it often, but when our mind is made up, even though someone or the group is still not in final agreement, you may hear us say, "Why? Name's on the door."

That's one way we use to transition from open discussion to definite decision and shift to the process of, "Now, how are we going to help make this happen successfully?"

When we walk out of the room with a decision made, there is no public dissent. No matter if there are still differing opinions, we're unified in how we're going to take action.

LESSON 65
How You See Is as Important as What You Say

We hope people know when one of us is serious, contemplative, encouraging, or pissed off. Each of these emotions may be necessary and useful in managing people. We think eye contact is important in all situations. Looking directly on when instructing; off into the distance when contemplative; lids wide open and embracing when encouraging; and focused, targeted, and/or penetrating when pissed off—each contributes to the message.

You can read a lot about when, where, and what body posture says and reflects during difficult and important conversations. But we're eye doctors, so we say concentrate on the eyes.

LESSON 66
We're Still Learning. Are You?

One of our favorite things in life is to learn from others—especially those who are experts in their fields. Perhaps that's why we like the concept of accelerated benchmarking (see lesson 61, "Accelerated Benchmarking—Outside Healthcare").

Dr. Jeff kids the staff all the time and says how much he likes being the dumbest person in the room. Somehow, they never disagree with his ability to achieve that! Hmm, maybe it's too obvious. The converse is true also. If someone else is doing a task regularly or is responsible for it, we figure they will know much more and communicate much more deeply on the subject than we can. In fact, if we don't see that type of deeper understanding, and if we feel like the smarter person on the subject, it perplexes and concerns us.

Truthfully, it sometimes frustrates us, as we believe that with active effort, any individual should be able to master an area of content and therefore should be able to readily answer the deeper questions on the subject. If they can't, perhaps they're not taking their responsibility seriously enough or are taking too passive an approach. We often want to delegate responsibility to people, but with responsibility comes obligation. Be entrusted and generate trust—or don't. It is an opportunity to grow.

One of the areas we seem to be relatively skilled in (or cursed with) is seeing, learning, or reading something from an entirely different industry and making it applicable to healthcare. That could be a *direct* transfer, like our airport scheduler boards (thanks to the Nashville International Airport), or a *similar* transfer like our online scheduling (from a bed-and-breakfast experience), or a *why not* transfer like Burger King orders and cycle time tracking.

Where most people say, incredulously, "How in the heck does that apply to us?" we see the direct applicability in many great systems devised by brilliant people in other disciplines. When we are traveling, we like to grab a magazine from a different area of science, industry, or hobby and see if there is anything we can learn and apply to make our office culture or care better.

> When we are traveling, we like to grab a magazine from a different area of science, industry, or hobby and see if there is anything we can learn and apply to make our office culture or care better.

We appreciate the eternal quest to improve and learn, and we have only scratched the surface. But we're still learning. And if you work in our office, you should be too.

LESSON 67
Once-a-Year Testing

Who is buried in Grant's Tomb? You know the answer. When should our glasses and contact lens patients have their next annual exam? You guessed it: one year from now.

Dr. Gary Gerber proposed a salient point to us: If we want to reinforce the importance and value of the yearly eye exam, then why do we only occasionally remind the patient? Remind them every step of the way.

Front desk staff: "Hi, Mrs. Smith. You are here for your *once-a-year* eye health exam."

Tech: "Mrs. Smith, come with me, and I'm going to do some of your *once-a-year* testing and get you ready for Dr. Keg."

Doctor: "And finally, Mrs. Smith, it was so good to see you, and I want to see you back next year for your *once-a-year* eye health and vision exam."

Checkout staff: "Have a great day, Mrs. Smith. It was great to see you, and here is your card for your [wait for it ...] *once-a-year* eye health and vision exam with Dr. Keg."

As we said earlier, courtesy of Dr. Jeff's dad, "No sinner was ever saved with one sermon. You have to remind them of important things over and over." True that, Dad, and thanks, Gary. See you in one year!

LESSON 68
He Takes a Shot and Scores!

We have so many wonderful patients. We often learn more from them than they do from us. Bobby Langley, a noted author and local basketball legend, broke down caring for us into a pretty simple, measurable, and attainable goal.

During one visit he said, "I love how you and your staff are so friendly, and I can tell you work at that." That, of course, made us feel really warm inside, as it validates that all of the hard work behind the scenes in hiring, training, and directing staff really does show.

He followed by suggesting this simple goal: "If you try to do one thing nice for someone every day, you will be successful."

Perhaps that doesn't sound like a stretch goal. Yet when you are sitting at home (or in the office) in the evening, reflecting on the day, can you always pinpoint the one nice thing you did for someone that day?

If so, and assuming that it occurs every day, that is at least 365 acts of personal kindness or niceness in one year. If we can rally our team of ten doctors and forty staff members to do the same, that is 18,250 nice things we do for people at our practice every year. In ten years, it's 182,500 nice things. Don't you think that some of those people will notice these kind acts? Certainly, your staff will feel a level of pride and fulfillment.

As hockey great Wayne Gretzky said, "You miss 100 percent of the shots you don't take." So take a shot at being nice on a daily basis, as Bobby suggests (he's a prolific scorer, himself, on the basketball court), and watch your business grow.

LESSON 69
Urban Meyer Units—As You Grow, Stay Small

As The Ohio State University graduates, we are big Buckeye fans. As such, we follow the Buckeyes on TV and still have season tickets to football games. We try to go to all the home games and even some of the away games every year.

However, there is no truth to the rumor that the entire staff must sing the Ohio State alma mater to receive a raise. Fight song, yes—alma mater, no! Actually, we love college football, period. There are great coaches in football, and the great ones distinguish themselves by building successful programs. We can learn a lot by copying them, modeling them, tweaking what they do, and introducing some of their methods into our practice. Sports program builders are great models for business builders.

We are fortunate to have had a great leader at Ohio State in Coach Urban Meyer. Like him (if you have him) or not (if you don't), you cannot argue with or have anything but respect for his success as a football coach. Coaching division one football is like running a business, a huge business. One of the methods we have learned from his approach is the breaking down of the team into component parts, or, as he calls them, units.

We have done the same thing, and it has merit, especially in a growing healthcare practice. One of the pitfalls of growth is that as you add more people, unless you continue to foster great team relationships, some people might get lost in the masses. We do not want that to happen. Indeed, one of the main ways we try to manage against that happening is by having our *all-member* strategic retreats and gap reviews as well as having weekly *all-member* staff meetings.

It is all too common in healthcare delivery that factions in a practice start acting out against each other. In eye care, you too often see it when the front office forms a clique versus the back clinical office. The front complains because sometimes the technical team has lulls in their patient care and stands around. The back complains that the front scheduled the wrong time for a patient or is insensitive to the special needs of a patient with a particular diagnosis. You get the picture—important at the moment, yet trivial really.

Good management and leadership breaks this down and constantly battles against this happening by keeping everyone focused on the bigger picture—care for patients. Every team contributes their part to a higher goal and definition of success. These goals are about patient flow and scheduling and access, patient satisfaction and loyalty, capture and conversion rate, and revenue and profitability. Most importantly, knowing how each team and team member contributes to the bigger goal by what they do.

As a noted expert consultant, Verne Harnish, once said in a meeting, "It has to show up on their day planner." In other words, the big picture is nice, but the role of each team member must be connected to the point that they see what they do every day connecting to and contributing to the bigger goal by witnessing it in their daily tasks.

So we need to have an overall strategy, plan, and goals—check.

We need to have each staff member engaged, motivated, and appreciated for the role they play—check.

We also need to have their team connected as a unit to the overall success of the bigger team. Ah, this is where Coach Meyer breaks his team down into component units or divisions. In his vernacular, it's the defensive backs, the linebackers, the offensive line, and so on.

In our practice, it is the front office team unit, the optical team unit, the doctor team units, and so on. Each has a set of mini mission goals that correlates to the practice's mission and goals but is more related to the daily tasks they do. It is the manager or team leader's goal to rally this unit so they connect to what their team unit should be producing, while at the same time not building a silo but keeping that unit connected into the bigger whole. That is a finesse, and it takes good leadership and management to accomplish. When it is accomplished, you can feel it, see it, and tangibly experience the teamwork. It is a beautiful thing, just like Buckeye football! Here is a graphic of how we have broken our practice into its component units, ala Coach Meyer, for better service and relationship-building delivery. We call it our twelve strong/five strong. Each person should know which units they are on and the goals for success for that unit.

Clarity of Purpose

CREATE THE BEST PATIENT EXPERIENCE EVER
"12 STRONG"

1 FRONT UNIT

Start the relationship. Greet, schedule and provide accuracy and access.

2 TECHNICAL UNIT

Build the relationship. Create trust, provide responsive, accurate and empathetic care.

3 DOCTOR UNIT

Cement the personal experience; care for person and eyes. Provide solutions.

4 OPTICAL UNIT

Create solutions, educate and match visual, functional and self image needs with optical product solutions.

5 MARKETING AND PATIENT LOYALTY UNIT

Recognize, create and appreciate loyalty. Tell our story and engage others to do the same in the community.

6 INSURANCE UNIT

Be responsive, accurate and quick in calculating and collecting payment.

7 ACCOUNTING UNIT

Provide accurate financial information needed for vendors, staff and owners to trust

8 CLINICAL UNITS

Connect patient needs to the best available preventative, palliative, medical and surgical optinos in care

9 INNOVATION/ DEVELOPMENT UNIT

Seek opportunities that expand or improve our care to and for others.

10 PVT UNIT

Improve vision and function through better optical and visual processing.

11 TCE UNIT

Improve athletic performance through eye-body function, prevent and rehabilitate injury to eye related processing

12 TIGER TRAINING UNIT

Educate and improve doctor, staff and patient knowledge. Share with others.

Clarity of Purpose

**CREATE THE BEST PATIENT EXPERIENCE EVER
PROTECT, PREVENT, CORRECT, AND ENHANCE
"5 STRONG"**

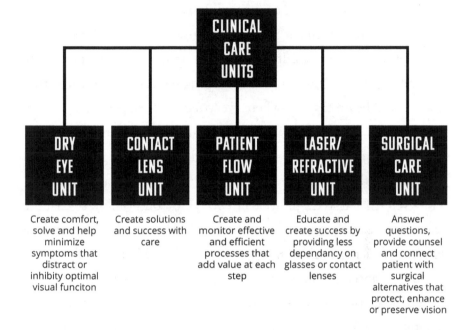

CLINICAL CARE UNITS				
DRY EYE UNIT	**CONTACT LENS UNIT**	**PATIENT FLOW UNIT**	**LASER/ REFRACTIVE UNIT**	**SURGICAL CARE UNIT**
Create comfort, solve and help minimize symptoms that distract or inhibit optimal visual funciton	Create solutions and success with care	Create and monitor effective and efficient processes that add value at each step	Educate and create success by providing less dependancy on glasses or contact lenses	Answer questions, provide counsel and connect patient with surgical alternatives that protect, enhance or preserve vision

LESSON 70
Heads Up—Make It Visible

Many people need visible reminders to retain information. In our office, visibility leads to sharing. Two areas stand out to us.

One, critical numbers in each department are important to track or graph to show trends. If we want the optical department to rally around a goal for a month, our daily progress toward achieving that goal should be on the wall where everyone in the department can see it. There is a lot of power in someone putting a dot on a graph and everyone monitoring it, being committed to seeing the goal achieved.

In any department, there are often many important indicators. However, strive to track just one or two critical ones visibly, so that the team understands what is *most* important. We're an IT society, and we love the efficiency of Excel tracking and graphs. Call us old school, but nothing connects a team member to a goal like personally placing a dot on a trend graph. That makes a real connection to its importance, which is something all managers try to accomplish with their team members.

Two, when a patient has a specific special need—this could be a patient for which we have made an error and we are redoing a job—that needs to be visible to more than just the person involved in Recovery (see lesson 108: "Treat the Person First, Then the Process—Recovery"). That particular job or patient is important to the entire department. Everyone should be aware of the priority and help to exceed the patient's expectations the second time. The use of "hot boards" (see lesson 71, "It's Getting Hot in Here") satisfies this need, and they are used routinely in our contact lens and optical departments.

Exceeding expectations and minimizing the chance of disappointing a patient a second time are great goals, and making tasks visible helps this happen. Visibility signifies importance.

LESSON 71
It's Getting Hot in Here

We use a "hot board" to signify and communicate special patient needs to our staff. This is simply a whiteboard with a patient's name, specific need, and date visible for all in the unit to see. We work hard to build systems of compassionate, responsive clinical excellence. That works great if each patient has predictable goals and expectations—that match what we want them to have.

Yet ask yourself, "How do you respond when a patient has an expectation greater than your typical ones or a unique need you could not have anticipated?"

This is a rubber-meets-the-road event that challenges every organization, and your response to it reflects your culture more than anything you say or preach.

To prepare for unique needs, one has to assume they will occur. We have to create a culture of responsiveness and train our staff to embrace the opportunity to accomplish a patient's special need, to own it, yet to *share that need* with other team members who might help. In this way, the need is watched by all, owned by one. And that's where the hot board comes in.

Accomplishing better-than-standard performance over time should be the expectation, yet it is only accomplished when a mix of good processes, communication, and people come together.

> Accomplishing better-than-standard performance over time should be the expectation, yet it is only accomplished when a mix of good processes, communication, and people come together.

First, the staff member's response of "here is what I *can* do for you" emphasizes never saying no without offering an alternative that we can say yes to (see lesson 19, "And I Would Do Anything for You, But I Can't Do That").

Second, does the team member feel the freedom to act, and are those actions reinforced by the practice culture? This is where examples and role playing come into play during staff training. It is also where weekly WOWs being communicated in front of all team members helps to establish norms. We may not have dealt with or practiced the exact patient need requested, yet we *have* discussed responding to things outside of typical requests.

Third, does one person own it?

Fourth, if a response by a certain time or date is needed, has that one person communicated the patient's needs to others in their department or in the office? This is where the hot board serves as a group awareness communication tool.

Fifth, it is important to reiterate the success when delivering it. Not in a bragging manner but to share in the joy of accomplishment with the patient—for example, "I wasn't sure we could get those lenses today, before you left on your cruise, but we worked hard with our staff and partner laboratory to prioritize them for you. I was so excited to call you when they arrived this morning and met our standards! Now you can see your best and look great on your trip!"

I am not naive to believe we can meet every special need and request. Yet building and fostering a mentality of *yes, we can do this* builds loyalty in the patient and pride in the staff. Keeping needs visible on a hot board potentiates this goal.

Meeting unanticipated needs with unexpectedly good results, having loyal patients and a staff that is proud and empowered—that is a double win!

LESSON 72
We Are in It for the Money—at Least Partially

There is not a business—and certainly not an optometry or oph-thalmology practice—that doesn't have a goal to make money. Don't fall prey to the comments from others that fall into one of these two categories:

1. "You work for a corporation, and all a corporation wants to do is make money." Well guess what, friends? All "anybody" wants to do in "any" business is make money. Show us a business that doesn't want to make money, and we will ask you why it's in business. People start businesses because they see an opportunity to make money or are driven by a cause and realize that to pursue that cause, they must be able to make money. Making money gives us the opportunity to pursue our goals, our purpose, and our mission.

2. "It isn't important how much money I make." Typically, these are doctors who are comfortable with the money they are already making in practice. Or they are doctors who just want to put in the minimum amount of effort and are afraid to work harder. In either case, the doctor has become com-placent. They don't desire to work harder and increase their stress level threefold for the purpose of making only a few more dollars.

Every business makes these types of value judgments. Whether you are a sole proprietor, in a partnership, work as an employee, or are an independent contractor with a corporation, we all sometimes make decisions that indicate it's not worth our effort for a small amount of return. Remember this when you hear doctors, in their most altruistic voice, say statement number one or two. We commend them on their success or condemn them on their laziness. However, if tomorrow their take-home pay was cut in half, do you believe they would still say making money doesn't matter? Unless they or their family had accumulated immense wealth, we believe they would be more concerned about making money at that point. Typically, the person who says, "I am not interested in making more money," has achieved a monetary reimbursement level consistent with their values and lifestyle, a level that varies for everyone.

The people who give the pursuit of money a bad name are those who push themselves, and others, over the limit and past the point of balance, so that the pursuit of money conflicts with basic moral values. They believe in making money at all costs, even if others may be hurt by their methods. This can create a true conflict for others, yet understand that it is not the pursuit of money *per se* that is at fault but, rather, that individual's value system. People with good moral values who are goal seeking, competitive, and want to improve themselves and others for the purpose of a cause can pursue the goal of making money without feeling guilty about it whatsoever.

At the age of eighty-three and wearing glasses for about fifty years it was the best visit I've ever had.

The staff was personable and human like the rest of us.

I especially appreciate how everything is explained and options are provided. I feel like I'm the most important person while at my appointment.

Unless I move I will never go anywhere else for my eye care.

Impressive efficiency with a personal touch.

This place is amazing!

CHAPTER 4

Focus on Developing, Building, and Nurturing a Culture

The fact is, culture eats strategy for lunch. You can have a good strategy in place, but if you don't have the culture and the enabling systems that allow you to successfully implement that strategy, the culture of the organization will defeat the strategy.

—Richard Clark, Merck & Co.

When interviewing someone, we often hear, "She's a Cool Springs EyeCare person," or "He's a Donelson type of guy; we should hire him." When you build an organization to the point where you pretty well can identify the type of person who will fit in well and succeed in the office, you have started to arrive at what Jim Collins called a "cult-like culture" in his book *Built To Last*.

Cults have, for many good reasons, a negative connotation. However, the development of who we are, why we are here, how we act, and what we intend to be, do, and get done is vital. Doctors, your culture represents you and contributes to your reputation. We each own our reputation and take pride in that. We work hard as a team of doctors and staff to be genuine, authentic, and consistent in who we are to all people. The last thing we would want is to be misrepresented or have someone act in conflict with our foundational beliefs. The following illustration shows the building blocks of our consistent care culture.

Creating a Culture of Consistency in Care

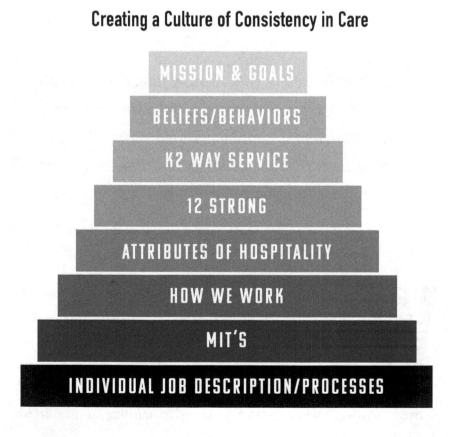

MISSION & GOALS

BELIEFS/BEHAVIORS

K2 WAY SERVICE

12 STRONG

ATTRIBUTES OF HOSPITALITY

HOW WE WORK

MIT'S

INDIVIDUAL JOB DESCRIPTION/PROCESSES

The pyramid reflects the components we feel are important to have in writing and communicated to each team member. It is our team leaders' management responsibility to know, demonstrate, and teach these to others. The culture of consistency pyramid represents staff alignment from individual role (day planner) to an organization's strategic mission (big picture).

We look for the type of people with character who will enhance our reputation. We do not try to hire all of the same people behaviors. That would be boring, generate a lack of innovation and growth, and ultimately, cause stagnation. We embrace differences, train in new and unique ways, yet insist that at the core, the people we have, the people we keep, and the people who lead us represent us in a way that enhances our reputation. That, we take pride in.

When you care about the patient and their experience, those culture-consistent people who embody your core values and attitudes are an essential component to building an office where it is fun to work and patients look forward to being seen.

LESSON 73
You Just Have to Demonstrate

Nothing we do as doctors or recommend to staff is successful unless we model what we preach. For that reason, how we greet patients and staff, provide care, remember personal things about patients, customize their eyewear choices, protect their vision with testing, and even how we laugh and joke with them—all represent our beliefs and care.

This goes especially for how we listen and recover from a mistake, when needed. We stress to our doctors that *we* set the tone for our care behaviors and standards. We need to do all of these things well. This is not a "do as I say, not as I do" practice. We think the humility of doctors shows through when they also practice the relationship-building service efforts we want every patient to experience.

LESSON 74
What We're Not Afraid Of

We are not afraid of our people growing smarter and more confident. We've heard some others say, "If you train your people too well, then you risk losing them to another doctor's office. Then you've wasted all of that time training for nothing." First, we live in a free and open environment—in most states, employees are at will. Anyone can leave (or be asked to leave) at any time and for any reason. We don't try to build walls or be protectionist and restrict knowledge so it can't be used against us. Rather, we are always striving to demonstrate our belief in our people, our desire to see them learn and grow, and our hope to make their job the best they'll ever have.

We do not fear training someone and losing them. We believe that if we want to help our people become better and surround them with a great atmosphere, we will keep them, more often than not. The staff will win as they grow in skills, behaviors, and confidence, and, above all, our patients will win by being well treated by our staff.

> We are always striving to demonstrate our belief in our people, our desire to see them learn and grow, and our hope to make their job the best they'll ever have.

WHAT WE WANT FOR OUR EMPLOYEES	HOW THIS HAPPENS
To show we believe in them	Managers and doctors communicate this to the staff who report to them and are cognizant of each staff member's long-term aspirational and short-term goals.
To see them learn and grow	This happens via managers, doctors, and trainers; staff meeting training; weekly and monthly training by department; Tiger Institute; after hours and during work; and leader and manager training. Also by putting specific training steps and/or courses into their annual employee plans. Further, by asking them where they'd like to grow to in our organization and creating a step-by-step plan on how to get there.
To make this the best job ever	This happens by creating and maintaining a positive culture in the office and by managing compensation and benefits, connecting what they do with the kind of patient care we provide and with the success of our business.

LESSON 75
Be Proud of the Appearance of Your Staff

Provide you staff with uniforms, and give them an annual allowance to purchase new uniforms, so that they are always wearing one that is clean and not outdated. When picking the colors, make sure they complement the decor in your office. If you're not good at picking colors, find someone in or out of the office to advise you. (We don't recommend red, by the way, as it psychologically amps up people's emotions.)

Healthcare is based on a trusting relationship. Shades of blue and green reflect trust. Social trends of accountability in appearance always evolve. When we were growing up, it was rare for a woman to have tattoos. Today, not so much. Personally, we don't judge, and we neither encourage nor discourage someone having tattoos. However, we *are* running a business. Having a business where people trust in us is important, and for that reason, we expect tattoos to be covered whenever possible. The same goes for alternate-area piercings. Again, we don't begrudge anyone who has them. But the simple fact is that our potential patients, who are putting their faith in us for a valuable and precious service, their eyesight, are always judging our competency, trustworthiness, and ability by how they perceive us. Appearance is important, and for that reason, we don't want anything that might detract from building a patient's level of confidence and trust in us.

LESSON 76
A Little Personalization Builds a Lot of Relationships

While we are on the subject of uniforms, try to add some practice personalization to your staff's uniform. This may be a button that tells the patient to ask the staff about a certain service or procedure you are featuring. It could also be a picture of the team member's family, parents, or kids. Perhaps it's a picture of the place they took their last vacation. Any addition to the standard uniform should look clean and uncluttered. Within appropriate bounds, it also gives your staff a chance to be proud. Let them show off something that represents their personal love and passions. Pay attention, and *you* may just learn something about your team members too!

These things give patients a reason to get to know you and your staff personally and to engage in conversation. Conversations begin to build trusting care relationships.

LESSON 77
Lanyards? The Staff Says No

In our quest to continually celebrate our staff's accomplishments and allow for patients to recognize them, we thought we should have pins to acknowledge certain milestones. Clinical certification, ten-year anniversaries, and service excellence are some of the many things that we are proud of our staff accomplishing. Give each staff member some pride by wearing pins that celebrate their accomplishments.

To have a place to put these pins, we settled on magnetic name tags hung on lanyards, which were bigger and more visible to patients and didn't need to be pinned to the uniform. We handed out the lanyards and new name tags with much fanfare. We talked about how we're developing pins that they could attach to the lanyards and then proudly display. The staff will love this right?

A swing—and a miss!

As the staff wore the lanyards, what we envisioned as a neat thing for them (who doesn't want to avoid pinholes in their scrubs or have to keep track of a name tag?) was perceived as a hassle by them. The lanyards got caught on desks. They interfered with technicians' work in the clinic. After some time, the staff resoundingly asked, "Can we go back to the name tags we had before?"

We relented. We never thought lanyards would be so polarizing. Every now and then, we'll kid our office manager and say, "Hey, I've been thinking of changing our name tags to lanyards again." The look in her eyes tells us she hasn't forgotten.

LESSON 78
Show Off Staff Accomplishments— Not Just Doctors'

At most doctors' offices, you'll see credentials posted on the wall. Impressive mahogany-framed diplomas in old English script displayed to reassure or impress patients with the doctor's credentials.

We're a team in our office, so we want the patients to see successful credentials achieved by *everyone* on our staff. CPO, CPOA, COA, NCLE, ABO, MBA—whatever is achieved by our staff gets recognized and celebrated.

We think it's great when our staff members take the time to challenge themselves, add to their education, and devote their time to achieving higher certification levels. So we support it by paying for study materials, and our doctors make themselves available to help staff prepare for exams and certifications. We've even put on our own courses through our Tiger Institute education division.

Did you pass the test? Congratulations! You'll get a bonus (higher amounts for higher levels), recognition in the staff meeting, and recognition that patients will see.

More importantly, *we* recognize and remember.

LESSON 79
You Want to Make What? We Want You to Make More!

We are never intimidated by knowing what staff members want to achieve financially in their lives. This aspirational goal drives them, whether they are open about it or not. Often, they have been told things like, "You'll never make that much—what a wild idea!" This squashes ambition, which is unfortunate.

We think it's important to know these financial goals, if the staff members will share them. Then our job becomes helping them with a path to reach those goals.

We had a staff patient transport driver once who made around $25,000 in the early 1990s. When we had this discussion, he told us he wanted to make $75,000. We told him, Great, how are we going to get you there? He did not have a plan; the number just sounded good to him. We told him he wasn't likely to get to that level just as a van driver, but if we created a transportation company as a side business and started transporting patients for other doctors also, it could happen. We also told him that an alternative, due to his great patient service attitude, was to grow into a role within the office and ultimately become a manager of one of our practices. That would be a different road for him to travel (no pun intended!), but it was a realistic way for him to make what he wanted.

We believed that if he was determined to make the amount of money he'd stated, he would either find a way in some other occupation not affiliated with us (bad for us as he had a career path here), or think about his job as more than just a driver and start to think about a transportation business. That way, he could grow our business as well as his own career. I'm not sure where he is now, but I hope that, by pushing him to grow in his career, he's making well over $75,000 now!

Our first job (and that of our leaders and managers) is to know what a team member wants and suggest to them whether that is achievable with us, and if so, how. We never want to squash anyone's dream of money made or position held. However, we often do have to help them with the realities of the work and sacrifice it will take to get to their goals.

That's okay with us, because we like goal-minded, high-aspirational people. That is also why we keep short-term training goals and long-term aspirational goals on a list for every person on our staff (see lesson 80, "Favorites—We Know What You Like"). We love it when we can help someone make what they want or do what they dreamed of, or, even better, grow them to make more or handle more than they ever thought was within their capability. We believe that stimulating that quality in our people is the ultimate win for us.

LESSON 80
Favorites—We Know What You Like

If you're going to look for ways to praise and reinforce great service behavior by a member of your staff, as we do, then PIC NIC (see lesson 88, "Have a PIC NIC") is the critical beginning. There are times that you want to give more recognition than a pat on the back or a friendly "way to go!" You want to give that team member something special. But what? Are they gluten free? Are they on a diet? Do they even like Starbucks coffee, and if so, what's their favorite drink there? Do they go to movies?

As we learn what our individual staff members enjoy, we keep such things on file and available for all to see. So, for example, if someone wants to thank Dr. Jeff or reinforce a behavior they like, they know they can get his attention with a Mars bar, Boston Baked Beans candy, coffee with cream, or anything Ohio State Buckeye football.

And, yes, we try to keep this information updated for every person on the team, doctors included. There are many excellent books and articles on reinforcing behaviors in your people. We emphasize some basic principles here:

1. Make it a "PIC NIC."

2. Know what they like.

3. Add emphasis by acting on and reinforcing what they like.

LESSON 81

Sometimes You Have to Demonstrate Over and Over—or Watch Dr. Susan!

We could have shortened this book with a simple mantra and recommendation. Just watch Dr. Susan. She is a model for the behaviors we recommend or insist on in care. Because of that, of course, her patients have fierce allegiance to her. Even when Dr. Jeff fills in (and he has the same last name), patients will inevitably look at him and say, "You're not her," or "Where is your wife?" When he says, "I am Dr. Susan's husband," they are polite, but he can tell he is only a humble student compared to the Jedi master!

What does she do so well? She genuinely cares. She is overtly friendly and does not project any air of doctor superiority. She is interested in the patient. She listens. She is direct in her recommendations and does not avoid the tough discussions. And she always leaves the room saying something amusing, such as, "See ya later, alligator."

She is a beacon of positivity and a model for other doctors on how to build trust and patient rapport. For that reason, it is important when we have new doctors or interns that we make sure they spend time with her. We can talk about how to care, yet there is no substitute for seeing it in action. Dr. Susan demonstrates it well, over and over.

Find the person in your office who does things well and use them as a natural teacher. "Say it, see it, now do it" is the training model that doctors (and staff) should subscribe to.

LESSON 82
The First Thing New Staff Members Should Hear

Your practice should be putting its best foot forward for new employees too. We will tell you this: the first thing new staff members should hear is *not*, "Here are the do's and don'ts from our legal department."

Think about it. When someone applies for a new job, they are anxious, curious, and hopeful. During the interview phase with us, they are learning about our company, our culture, and our mentality of care. They are trying to determine if this is a good fit for them, and we are trying to determine if they are a good fit for us. They become hopeful, even excited. Nervous excitement and hopefulness yields to true excitement and relief when they are offered the job and accept. Then, excited anticipation sets in as they prepare for the transition into a new workplace, filled with new people—all of whom know their jobs, while the new person does not. But they are excited to fit in, to excel, and to help us succeed.

The first thing they should experience is an elevation of that excitement by reinforcing how happy we are that they have joined us and how many great opportunities there are for growth within our organization. Essentially, a reinforcement that they made the right decision.

Sure, the legal stuff is vital and important, yet it should never be the first thing someone experiences when they are starting a new career with us. Think about our and your process for onboarding—especially the first day. What would *you* like to hear, see, and experience? Our goal is for that new person to go home even more confident that they made the right decision than when they entered that morning.

LESSON 83

We Are Not Closing Today; We Are Getting Ready to Open Tomorrow

Each area of the practice has an opening and a closing procedure. Each area has a staff member who is responsible for opening and closing. We like to tweak the mentality of the last jobs of the day. You see, we really are not closing today. We are actually preparing to open tomorrow.

The more you adopt this mentality, the less carryover you will have, and the less you will hear, "We'll do it tomorrow" or "We'll finish that later."

Preparing to open tomorrow has significant connotations. Everything must look good and be ready for patient care. Even though there is an opener, that person will have limited duties if the previous night's opening readiness was performed well. It sets a tone of starting the day prepared.

LESSON 84
Doctors Don't Talk Fees

In our practice, we seek, hire, and keep good doctors. Good doctors are good people. Good people are compassionate people. Compassionate people make great partners in business. They inherently reflect our caring and beliefs. Doctors demonstrating these qualities are important for staff and patients to see.

There *is*, however, a tragic flaw to this approach too. Caring doctors sometimes want to give away services or "help" patients get the best insurance deal. In their minds, this is part of the altruism in care, yet it's not good for business.

> Compassionate people make great partners in business. They inherently reflect our caring and beliefs.

Therefore, here's our rule: doctors don't talk fees. Simple rule, hard to learn and reinforce, yet vital. Doctor's *should* have a good understanding of what something costs and a general understanding of what is reimbursed. But we can't know everything: insurance deductibles, outstanding balances, copays, and so on. In our well-meaning, compassionate approach, we are too often misquoting fees or amounts a patient will have to pay. When this happens (and it does), the patient says what every front office collection person, office manager, or insurance person hates: "That's not what the doctor told me it would be!" Strike up the Caring Alert and Recovery (see lesson 108: "Treat the Person First, Then the Process—Recovery"). This takes time, thought, staff energy, and sometimes a reduction in the reimbursement. How do we avoid this?

It's simple: doctors, don't talk fees!

LESSON 85
We Almost Never Celebrate the Person Who's Leaving

Once someone is leaving—and we mean leaving for a similar job in the same profession or position somewhere else in town—our attention focuses forward. We will not stand in the way of someone bettering themselves with a new promotion, better pay, or more responsibility. We *will* talk to them to make sure they have considered *all* aspects of the comparative job and not just the amount of pay. As we mention in lesson 102, "Rehiring Previous Employees," they don't get the chance to say, "Sorry, made a mistake, I'm coming back." You leave and we're still friends, but you can't come back and work here.

Despite being a small business, we may make a decision to cut the departing employee's notice period short. We don't want the distraction of that person potentially making other staff members second-guess their position or happiness. That's unnecessarily kicking a sleeping dog.

Further, when they leave, we thank them for their contribution and wish them well. But no cakes, celebrations, parties, parting gifts, or anything like that at the office. We're not happy they are leaving, so we're not celebrating losing a good person.

Further, we are far more focused on the people we still have, those who are on our team, rather than those who aren't. On *Shark Tank*, Kevin O'Leary says, "You're dead to me." We're not that harsh, but our minds don't dwell on who we had; we dwell on who we have.

LESSON 86
Moments of Truth in Clinical Care

Part of onboarding new doctors and staff members is a section on patient flow and service called moments of truth. Jan Carlzon, former president of Scandinavian Airlines, coined the phrase *moments of truth* for that moment when the customer is looking you eye to eye. Those moments count more than others in shaping the customer's (or patient's) impression of overall care.

We created and show staff members a video on how to correctly manage these moments of truth. A little instruction and scripting goes a long way in these important areas. While we cannot include the video for each person to see in this book, we can give you an idea of how we introduce the concept, teach, train, and reinforce the expected methods and behaviors. Want to make an improvement in the patient's overall impression of their experience? Discuss with your team your own moments of truth and start with a good understanding of what should happen at each moment.

Introduction to the Moments of Truth

Thank you for joining us on an important learning experience as we discuss the moments of truth in the clinical office setting. Moments of truth are those critical moments in your practice when patients are shaping their impression about your overall care. You might be wondering how we decided what makes up a moment of truth. We asked and listened! Through focus groups and satisfaction surveys, we asked patients what they need and want out of their visit to the doctor. Patients told us to do the following:

Treat them with respect.

Listen to them.

Give clear explanations and easy instructions.

Send a bill they can understand.

Moment One: Telephone Greeting

Recommended Moment for Reference

"Good morning," [name of practice]. This is [name of person]. How may I help you?"

The staff member smiles and uses clear words and a warm and friendly tone.

Moment Two: Check-In

Recommended Moment for Reference

Immediately when a patient enters the building, the employee makes eye contact, smiles, and greets the patient (by name if possible).

Moment Three: Call to the Clinic

Recommended Moment for Reference

"Hi, Mrs. Jones, I am [name], and I will be taking care of you today." (This occurs at the patient's chair.)

The employee introduces themself to the patient and other family members. The staff member smiles and uses clear words and a warm and friendly tone, and then they walk to the patient and stay with them en route to the workup area.

Moment Four: Introduction to the Doctor

Recommended Moment for Reference

The doctor briefly reviews the chart outside the exam room door.

The doctor then enters the room, states the patient's name, makes eye contact, and smiles.

The doctor introduces themself to the patient and family members with a friendly handshake (or, if social distancing, an elbow bump).

Moment Five: Explanation of Clinical Findings and Plan
Recommended Moment for Reference

Restate the patient's name.

Restate the chief complaint.

State your findings.

Discuss treatment options and recommended treatment plan. Ask if the patient or family members have any questions. Provide a handout if it exists. Write down medication dosage and frequency. Walk the patient to the next stop.

Moment Six: Reiteration of Clinical Findings and Plan
Recommended Moment for Reference

The employee makes eye contact and leads the patient out of the exam room. Both parties stop at a designated area, where the scribe reviews what the doctor recommended and prescribed. The scribe also asks the patient if they have any questions. Customized educational handouts are given to support the diagnosis and/or recommended treatment or testing. The scribe walks with the patient to optical, checkout, or next point of care.

Moment Seven: Checkout
Recommended Moment for Reference

When a patient checks out, ideally, they will be greeted with a smile, have their charges reviewed, and make a follow-up appointment. If those steps are met, the moment of truth has been successful. In our office, we have an additional necessary step—to fill out a quick checkout survey.

Moment Eight: Receipt of Bill

Recommended Moment for Reference

The bill should be clear, legible, and easy to understand.

A phone number and email address should be readily visible on the bill in the event the patient has questions and needs to contact the office. Even better are instructions so the patient can text to discuss the charges, pay by Venmo, or pay online.

To say that they have great customer service is an understatement.

Probably the best experience I've had when going to an eye doctor.

Top-notch place. I go to them even though they are not in my network.

Did not feel rushed at all and all of the charges were carefully explained to us. We will definitely be back!

Would never go anywhere else.

First-class operation! Everyone treats you with respect.

CHAPTER 5
Focus on Our People and Behaviors

Come to the edge.
We might fall.
Come to the edge.
It's too high!
Come to the edge!
And they came
And he pushed
And they flew.

—Christopher Logue, "New Numbers"

I f leadership is a process and human resources are a process, then success comes best when both are aligned.

Many books are written on the most valuable asset in a company being its people. It seems everywhere we lecture, consult, or discuss building a business, people management is responsible for the greatest amount of manager time, energy, and often, frustration.

"Why can't I just tell them once and have them do it?" That is a common new manager complaint, until they learn that consistency in behavior requires repetition in message.

That takes time. There is no easy way to develop your staff. However, there sure are a lot of wrong ways!

Let's start with a few basics that we believe.

You can train skills yet only modify behaviors and attitudes. It sure is nice when you hire a person with both skills and the right attitude and behavior! Sometimes great people just fall in your lap. There are times when the person is good yet just doesn't fit your organizational culture. Don't take it personally. (Although even today after many years, it is hard not to.)

A higher turnover is generally a problem with your hiring, training, or management. Sometimes all three. So don't be myopic and believe that one benefit, improvement, or new idea will fix the personnel turnover problem. Look at each area and assess your processes.

Believe in your people; care about them; and learn about them, their hopes, dreams, and desires, and, yes, flaws or insecurities. We all have them, even doctors. Okay, especially doctors!

Past behavior is the best predictor of future behavior. When hiring, ignore this at your own risk.

Know your ABCs. To understand this concept in more detail, read Aubrey Daniels's classic book *Performance Management*.

Encourage more than criticize.

Expect more in people's ability, capacity, growth potential, and behaviors.

People's work behaviors are often cultivated by past experiences in jobs, and those often need to be overcome.

We often have to overcome a person's long-held beliefs and insecurities about themselves, and we may be the first people who truly believe in them and want them to achieve. That takes time, yet look for those sparks of enthusiasm, as they will grow.

Appreciate loyalty—not blind loyalty, but those that trust your judgment, wisdom, insight, perspective, and experience. These people make you better.

Spend more time on people management, training your leaders more than any other task.

Discuss issues openly and counsel managers. You had to learn by making mistakes. So do they. People management and team building are the toughest part of management; it is for you, and it will be for them. Support, help, and grow your leaders to believe in the contributions of the whole person, not the actions of a single event.

We tell everyone that we want this to be the best job they ever had. We truly mean that. Yet we don't just want them to throw a log on our fire (culture). We want them to grow the fire by always being fire starters.

Friction, though difficult to handle and manage, like a soap bubble, displays only beauty and color through its interference.

Some of our greatest feelings of satisfaction and pride are in the people who have grown and contributed and now maintain positions of more authority and influence than they ever thought possible. Those are our wins! Relish them, for your measurement of success is the inner feeling, not an external metric.

Surround yourself with people you like. And be one of those people whom others like. Say hi and make a positive impact on your people's lives.

In the words of rap poet Biggie Smalls, "And if you don't know, now you know."

LESSON 87
Praise Frequently—but Know When and Where

One of the most important parts of management is allowing your employee to maintain or enhance their self-esteem. Remember this rule. Say it to yourself over and over again—and don't break it. Praise your employees and colleagues frequently, but do it when and where it's appropriate. The when is easy—as soon as you can, to connect the great act you're praising with the time it happened. The where is as important and requires leaders to understand their employees' and colleagues' personalities.

> Praise your employees and colleagues frequently, but do it when and where it's appropriate.

Extroverts love public praise and relish being celebrated with a staff meeting WOW! Celebrate their accomplishments out loud and in front of others. Thanking them in a staff meeting for a job well done energizes them.

Introverts tend to be embarrassed and less comfortable with public praise. They typically prefer the individual pat-on-the-back or thank-you gesture in private. These are more energizing to them. Personal cards work wonders for their energy.

Neither extroverts nor introverts enjoy being called out in public for mistakes they've made. Don't do it. Ever. And if it does happen, apologize in public too. Everyone on the staff needs to know that this is not acceptable behavior.

LESSON 88
Have a PIC NIC

One of the most valuable lessons in people management we have learned through reading over our careers is to always have a PIC NIC.

No, not the type that requires a park bench, blankets, watermelon, wine, and a bucket of chicken!

In *Performance Management*, Aubrey Daniels stresses the subtle yet very important approach to providing feedback. We'll summarize our understanding and implementation of what he says, briefly:

For maximum effect, make your feedback Immediate and Certain (as opposed to delayed and uncertain).

We want the recipient to know exactly what they did (well or not) as close to the event as possible. Add in that this can be **P**ositive (or constructive), **I**mmediate, and **C**ertain feedback (**PIC**) or **N**egative, **I**mmediate, and **C**ertain feedback (**NIC**), and you see where the acronym we use comes from.

We hope that our existing managers (and soon, new and growing managers) don't need a long review of Mr. Daniel's teachings. We can remind them of the importance of giving timely feedback just by saying, "Who has had a PIC NIC lately?" or "Are you going on a PIC NIC?" Sometimes we may comment on an employee performance dilemma with, "I agree with you about Sallie's work—I find PIC NICs to be helpful here."

We never met Mr. Daniels, but if we had, we'd have thanked him for PIC NICs.

LESSON 89
Don't BS Us, Cuz We Won't BS You

If we tell you we're pleased, we're pleased. If we tell you we're frustrated, we're frustrated.

God gave us a pretty good ability to think on the fly, maybe even negotiate or schmooze some, but we're not going to lie or BS you. So please don't BS us. If you're happy, tell us; confused, tell us; mad, tell us. Don't ever look us in the eyes and tell us one thing, only to go and tell others something different.

Respect means being direct, not hurtful, yet having the ability to be open in communication and dialogue. We pledge that we won't ever intentionally tell you one thing, then go tell others another. We all can change our minds over time, we admit. We're not talking about that. We're talking about things like saying, "Yes, Dr. Jeff" to his face and "No, Dr. Jeff" to others. We can't accept or understand that.

How fatiguing it must be for people who just tell others what they want to hear or, especially, act one way to one person and another way to another. How can they keep track when balancing two personalities? Nice to the boss, mean to others. Better to just be nice (and the same) to everyone.

We like open, direct conversations aimed at improving people care or systems. NO BS.

LESSON 90
Don't Take It Personally

There are a few jerk bosses or colleagues out there who make it a point to reprimand others in a personally attacking manner. We don't. Spencer Johnson and Kenneth Blanchard said it best in *The One Minute Manager*: "The first goal in correcting a person's behavior, whether by redirect, reprimand or praise, is to build or maintain the person's self-esteem." The person should never question their worth or value as a human being, ever.

As people who like to teach, we have found that often, when we're instructive and want to improve things, just our pointing out potential improvements can make people feel hurt or frustrated. We've seen it more often than we'd like. While this could be due to the recipient not having received constructive criticism before, or having been in a "screw up and you're fired" fear-filled job in the past, we suspect it's something in our body language that's speaking louder than what we say. If you have also experienced this unintentional reaction, our advice is to learn from it, be aware, and attempt to treat all people with respect. You can't avoid reprimands, and you shouldn't avoid trying to help people improve. At some point, most people will understand that your motives are sincere and that communication and feedback are a part of the office culture. Only then can trust develop.

It's a lot easier to *avoid* teaching or reprimanding someone, but, in the long run, that's self-defeating. People don't grow, and therefore, your organization doesn't grow. When you must instruct someone or change the way they do something, remember first to remind them of how valuable they are and what a good job they do. Share with them your goal of wanting to improve things to make things better for everyone.

If you are on the receiving end of criticism or advice, it's important not to take it personally. If you do something wrong and someone points this out, you can be frustrated, but you should never question your worth. If someone says something that you perceive to be personally attacking, rather than behavior modifying, it's important for you to stand up to them and say something. "Hey, Joe, I think I hear what you're saying, but you really seem to be attacking me personally. Is that really the way you meant it?" You'll find that this simple statement generally stops the criticizer and his personal attack in its tracks. Most people care about how someone feels and will apologize immediately if their message has been misperceived. We do. If we are instructing, reprimanding, *or* just talking about how we can improve things, don't take it personally, and we won't either.

LESSON 91
Those Who Trust and Those Who Don't

People generally tend to fall into two personality types: those who are initially trusting and those who are not. Those who are initially trusting will be loyal and buy into the mission immediately. They will act in concert with you, unless you create confusion or conflict between the way you talk and the way you walk. Appreciate these people for the trust they put in you and the practice. The security these people have in giving that trust freely should never be underestimated or taken advantage of. It's your job to reinforce and deepen their loyalty.

Those who don't trust you will need to be convinced. This will take time—and we can't tell you how long. It depends on the clarity of the mission you have presented, whether day-to-day activities and behaviors support and reinforce that mission or differ with it. It is important for you as a manager and leader to know when people who are initially apprehensive need more training and more encouragement to trust. Once these people surpass that threshold of trust, they are usually deeply committed. It is very important for you to recognize when a person who is inherently distrustful becomes trusting. It is conversely important for you to recognize when a person who is distrustful is disloyal. No amount of encouragement, teaching, or experience will sway their views. Those people need to find a different practice, because their personal mission will differ too significantly from your mission.

We have generally found, however, that the people who *chronically* distrust other people's motives or intentions are usually the people *you* shouldn't trust.

LESSON 92
How You Listen and Respond Is as Important as What You Do

Look the person you're talking to in the eye, and accept praise and encouragement by saying, "Thank you." You also need to stay focused with your eyes when someone is contemplating, yet say nothing, letting them think. If you're being criticized, corrected, or disciplined, you need to maintain good eye contact in an accepting, nondenying way and say nothing. Only when you know the reinforcer is finished and there is a pause can you (and should you) say, "I'm sorry. You're right; I should do better, and I will."

In these critical feedback conversations, uncomfortable as they can be, it is important for the speaker to hear and know they have been heard. Eye contact should go both ways.

One of our best ever managers used to listen but not make eye contact or vocally reinforce that she understood us—or even heard us. That not only frustrated us but also seemed to amp up our rhetoric and cause us to talk more—to be *really* sure she heard and understood us.

When we finally talked about this, she admitted that, as an introvert, she tends to just listen and then needs to think about it before saying anything. We explained that we never thought about it that way and acknowledged that she nearly always did address the issue and fix whatever needed correcting. We told her that, despite her natural tendencies, it would help us (and her) to look at us, acknowledge she'd heard, and *then* think about corrective actions.

This conversation helped all of us. She learned what we needed, and we better understood her. We don't have too many tense conversations (she's one of the best!), yet when we do, I think we now come out of it with each of us understanding the other better.

LESSON 93
And One Reviews

We think it's important to have performance reviews. We try to separate them from pay adjustments. If we don't, then the whole time the employee is sitting there hearing blah, blah, blah and thinking only, "Will I get a raise; will I get a raise?"

We expect team leaders to coach and be in contact with their direct reports every day, week, and month. No annual performance review should be a surprise to the employee being reviewed. If it is, we assume first that it's due to poor communication on the part of our manager.

In addition to the reviews and being in frequent contact with the team, we've introduced a more formal, albeit brief, review discussion we call the *And* One. Where did we get that? From an old basketball shoe company that had traveling basketball games with local stars competing with a national group of players. So does that mean we challenge each of our team members to a one-on-one game or a three-point shooting contest on the basketball floor? (We *do have* a basketball court in our office for sports vision training, you know!) Nope, we just adopted the name *And* One because it represented what we wanted each manager to communicate and each staff member to hear.

What is an *And* One? It's a simple method whereby the manager sits in a three- to five-minute meeting with a team member and says, "Mary, one thing you do really well that I appreciate is [X]. And one thing I would like you to work on [improve on, stop doing, do more, do less] is [X]."

A short discussion, and then they're done. *And* Ones are valuable when done right because they are brief and recognize both an area of strength and an area or opportunity to improve. They teach managers to be comfortable having both types of conversations with employees, and we find that to be a very valuable training exercise. Certainly, it's better than the once-a-year awkwardness of only a performance review. Our intended minimum formal discussions between team leader and team member may look like this:

> *And* Ones are valuable when done right because they are brief and recognize both an area of strength and an area or opportunity to improve.

January 1: Annual performance review

April 1: *And* One

August 1: *And* One

January 1: Next annual performance review

LESSON 94
No Sinner Was Ever Saved with One Sermon

Early in his career, Dr. Jeff received wise counsel from his personal sensei, his dad. Jeff would say something like, "I told them how we wanted this done. Why didn't they do it right? Did they forget?"

To his chagrin, his dad would ask questions such as, "Did you remind them?" "When did you last review this with them?" "Did you role-play it?" "Have you seen them doing it well and reinforced it with a positive comment?" "Have you seen it done poorly and corrected it?"

Early on, and truthfully, still now sometimes, Dr. Jeff responds with, "Ugghhh, that takes so much time! No, I haven't. Why don't they just get it?" Then he reconsiders and realizes that, like everyone else, he has a lot of things on his mind, a number of methods or processes he's trying to remember and master. Therefore, it takes time. Management is about continuing to be the drumbeat, the reinforcer—even when you'd rather just cut to the chase, say it once, and be done. We have to admit, our parents still continue to find ways to look smarter and smarter with time! Thanks, Dad.

Often, now *we* serve as counselors, trying to help our team leaders and doctors to not just introduce a topic but to reintroduce it, remind people about it, and find new ways to help others understand and practice consistently. Will you remember every lesson in this book? No! But if we concentrated on a few key lessons and worked on only those before moving on to others, we would see those points embedded and become habits.

Dr. Jeff's father also reminds us that it is important to train not just for training's sake but to focus on things that will have an impact. And, ideally, there should be a measurable method of evaluating whether the training was successful. Uggghhhh! How time consuming, yet you know, he's right. No sinner was ever saved with one sermon!

LESSON 95
Your Skills Are Great, Yet We Expect More

Most medical and optometric practices (and businesses too) have skill improvement as the most important measure of success. Furthermore, the increased skills may be the rational or most important element in deciding on raises. We agree that skills are important. Yet if we expect more from our people than only developing their skills, then we ought to review their performance on more than a *skills-only* scale, right? Right! And we do.

Our people in all areas of the practice are evaluated more wholly on their performance. We break these down into five key areas; PS, S, T, V, and C.

PS—Patient Service: Our reputation, differentiation, and success are built on this fundamental. Interpersonal skills, friendliness, responsiveness, and follow-up are each components of this evaluation. How often are you mentioned in the staff meeting with WOWs from staff for patient actions? How many POWs do you suggest and comment on? In patient surveys, are you mentioned by name? Do the doctors hear positive comments from patients about you as a staff member? Do you embody our principles, values, and behaviors (many of which are listed in this book)? And are you looking for ways, making suggestions, and helping implement ideas to improve care and service to patients? Are you involved in small pilot PDSA innovation cycles?

S—Skills: These are the core components of what and how you do your job. Do you understand your most important tasks? Do you perform them flawlessly and continuously? Can we trust the results of tests you perform? Can we trust your ability to follow a process and perform your job with less need for oversight? In essence, can we trust you to do your job as expected and well? Do you look for ways to add to your known skills? Are you trying to learn new skills and roles and understand the interrelationship of your skill output with other positions' needs? Do you attend and actively participate in extra training opportunities?

T—Teamwork: Too often in business, we see talented people who don't play well with others. It's a shame. In many medical practices, the more highly skilled a person is, the less they may be willing to help others. Unfortunately, they are often tapped to be managers, despite not possessing the inherent team-building mentality so critical to success in management. Some of these skilled people seem to forget that others helped them learn along the way. Some may even resist helping others, so as to maintain their "best" title. So shortsighted (especially if it occurs in an eye-care practice!). Teamwork is observable. We can see it when it's there and especially when it is not. Doctors and managers evaluate teamwork as it relates to them and their team units getting things done. We go one step further. We do a teamwork survey one to two times per year, then score and trend the results. Here is an example of the survey results:

OPTOMETRY OFFICE STAFF TEAMWORK SURVEY—SAMPLE

Please evaluate your other staff members in the following behaviors and rate them as follows:

4 = Always

3 = Very often

2 = Occasionally

1 = Rarely

0 = Never

N = Not enough experience with the person in this behavior to fairly provide an impression

	MANAGER	TECH	OPTICIAN	RECEPTION	INSURANCE
Polite and respectful to other staff members	3.8	3.8	3.2	4.0	3.8
Polite and respectful to patients	4.0	4.0	3.6	4.0	3.8
Willing to help a coworker when asked	3.2	4.0	3.0	4.0	4.0
Volunteers to help in other areas	3.2	4.0	2.6	4.0	3.8
Displays a positive attitude in the practice	3.4	4.0	2.6	4.0	3.8

Promotes good teamwork in the office	3.0	(4.0)	2.8		(4.0)		(4.0)	
Is someone I trust	2.8	(3.8)	2.0		(3.8)		3.4	
Is willing to do extra to help patients	(4.0)	(4.0)	3.2		(4.0)		(4.0)	
Displays highly ethical behavior	3.4	3.8	3.0		(4.0)		3.8	
Strives for excellence in their work	3.2	(4.0)	2.8		(4.0)		(4.0)	

high scores circled, low scores underlined

Each person gets a survey and has the ability to evaluate every person on staff. This method of extra objective input often surprises new staff members. First, it requires trust. Trust that we will use the information and feedback to be honest and open with our people. Ever know a person who sucks up to or schmoozes their boss, yet is short or disrespectful, perhaps even rude, to others on staff? Yeah, me too. The teamwork survey helps us uncover that. You may fool your doctor, you may fool your manager sometimes, but you can't fool your fellow team members. Teamwork counts. We expect it, and we test for it.

V—Versatility: While the teamwork section reviews the relationship with people in your unit, on your team, or those in other areas of the practice, we want staff who seek to help out and learn tasks in other areas. Versatility is value. It shows you have initiative. It shows a willingness and want to learn all parts of the business. It prepares people to take on more responsibility and grow in scope and compensation. It also demonstrates our spirit, commitment, and values by being willing to help out in any area where there is a need. That saves money too! And it provides better patient service.

In every business or office, there are a few core skills that we'd like each person to be able to know and master. We have defined those and encouraged our leadership team to allow their people time to invest in mastering the versatility skill basics. In essence, we've said, "Here is what you need to do and what it takes to score high on the versatility part of your review. We want you to score well." We have defined success and provide the opportunity (with encouragement by managers) to accomplish it.

C—Certification: In every job there are opportunities to get extra training, advance in your skills, and sometimes to become certified. Two of our most outstanding office managers have gone so far as to becoming certified in technical areas outside their own scope or role. Want to squash the excuse by a person that certification takes too long, is too hard, is not needed? Show a medical technician an office manager who has become certified two levels above them. Wow. Show a noncertified optician an office manager who pursued and accomplished board certification as an optician. Wow. The type of individual who challenges themself to learn, know, grow, and possess knowledge so it can help them and their team better manage and work, admittedly, is rare and special. They are also appreciated for their demonstrated commitment to additional training.

We believe in certification from outside credentialing bodies. We pay for the training and the testing and, once the staff member is certified, give a monetary bonus as an achievement congratulations. Being certified though is not the end-all. Many times, we have encountered well-skilled and well-trained (certified) technicians coming from other offices who ascribe to the belief that "I'm good because of my skills and credentialed qualifications." They are sometimes surprised (shocked) to hear skills are important yet not the only criteria upon which success is judged. The good ones get it and actually relish this. They understand, and just as they sought to succeed in their skills training, they challenge themselves to achieve excellence in the other areas of PS, T, and V. Pursuing well-rounded excellence across this broader spectrum of evaluation prepares them for growth as leaders in the practice. These are the people we seek. They set a higher bar. Those who think the overall grading scale is unfair and only skills should count, well, they will find either somewhere else that fits them better, or we inevitably will need to free their future. Culture counts, and evaluating our people in all areas that matter counts. Make sure how you review your people is consistent with the culture, goals, and the behaviors you want to encourage.

LESSON 96
What Is Your Value?

If you like the concept of evaluating your people (doctors included) on more than just skills, how do you communicate and implement it?

We like using a concept most of our people can relate to—beer! It's not PBR but rather **PVR**—the personal value ratio.

Imagine two staff members in the technical area of the practice:

1. **Jimbo** is a rising star, according to his team leader. He can work up and special test and is now scribing. He is learning to refract, and he has observed in PVT/TCE with the intent to be able to provide help there when needed. He comes to work on time every day and is jovial with other members of his unit. Other team members have commented on how willing he is to anticipate or help out when they get behind and need assistance. Importantly, patients love him and have frequently commented about his "conversational empathy and listening skills." He answers phones and greets in the front when cancellations occur and is learning to adjust and dispense. He is pursuing his CPO.

2. **Gus** is an experienced ophthalmic assistant, having previously worked in optometric and retinal offices. He can work up, do all special tests, scribe, refract, assist in surgery, help in tech on call, and evaluate contact lenses on the doctor's schedule or independently. Unfortunately, Gus seems to have more flat tires than other staff members. He frequently calls in sick or with car problems, thus forcing an overhaul of tech duties in the unit. He sits at TOC but shows little initiative, and other team members say he is lazy. He has to be asked to help in the front or optical and begrudgingly goes. Patients say "meh"; they

don't complain but don't have a lot of positive comments about their interactions with Gus. No doubt he knows his stuff and is COA, COT, COMT, NCLE, and CPOT certified.

Instead of evaluating just on the skills, in which Gus would excel, we rate the staff member's value on a more comprehensive performance metric scale:

PVR

PS: 30 percent

S: 30 percent

T: 20 percent

V: 15 percent

C: 5 percent

Each area is graded on a one-to-ten scale and then multiplied by the percentage ratio. Gus scores particularly high in the S area, yet Jimbo contributes value more in other areas. Each of these hypothetical ophthalmic assistants end up with different value grades based on the overall rating scale in place.

PVR "RISING STAR"	PVR "MR. EXPERIENCE"
PS 30% x 9 = 2.7	PS 30% x 4 = 1.2
S 30% x 4 = 1.2	S 30% x 9 = 2.7
T 20% x 10 = 2.0	T 20% x 1 = 0.2

V 15% x 8 = 1.2	V 15% x 4 = 0.6
C 5% x 0 = 0	C 5% x 10 = 0.5
PVR = 7.1	**PVR = 5.2**

To be effective, each of the areas should be defined as much as possible. Every team member needs to know how good value performance is evaluated in each area rated. Doctors, managers, and administrators need to think deeply about what areas are defined as important, what defines excellent performance, and then, who is providing true value to the organization.

One More Consideration

What if I told you Jimbo, the *rising star*, was being paid $12 per hour, and Gus, *Mr. Experience*, was making $16 per hour?

Here is how a lead team manager might look at this. Say each one point on the scale is hypothetically worth $2.5.

Jimbo: PVR of 7.1 x $2.5 = $17.75 vs. current pay of $12 per hour

Gus: PVR of 5.2 x $2.5 = $13 vs. current pay of $16 per hour

Who is more valuable according to the PVR? Both want a raise.

1. Who would you more likely give it to?

2. How would you counsel Jimbo?

3. How would you counsel Gus?

4. What other thoughts or considerations do you have in this hypothetical PVR example?

I see many practices that continue to raise skilled people to high enough levels that they end up having nowhere to go to improve in compensation or responsibility. The multievaluation method keeps employees aimed toward what owners really want—more value from employees than what they are paid. Paying equal to value is a prescription for financial losses. You are investing in your people. Help them grow and make more or take on more responsibility. That investment, like any other piece of equipment or new service, should pay off in return on investment in multiples. Let's be real. That is what business is all about. Frankly, we, too, better be providing much more of a value contribution to the organization than what our salaries as owners indicate, or we need to find someone else to run the company.

LESSON 97
How Much Do You Weigh?

You know the reception room exists, but the waiting room doesn't (see lesson 6, "It's a *Reception* Area"), yet there are times when a "weight" is important. It is important to us in deciding on a staff member's PVR.

We choose to stress five components, but all are not weighted equally. For instance, we showed how we weigh the components for our technical ophthalmic assistant people:

PS: 30 percent

S: 30 percent

T: 20 percent

V: 15 percent

C: 5 percent

This may be different and change when evaluating the insurance team:

PS: 20 percent

S: 40 percent

T: 15 percent

V: 15 percent

C: 10 percent

Or for our opticians:

PS: 35 percent

S: 35 percent

T: 15 percent

V: 10 percent

C: 5 percent

It is up to the business leader to determine what the components are and the appropriate weighting for the organization and its people.

LESSON 98
You Can't Buy Loyalty

Our experience says that someone who is a good producer but whose loyalty you question should not be given more responsibility to influence. Raising their authority level managerially is inappropriate. It reinforces the very attitude you do *not* want in the rest of your staff. This rewards the successful accomplishment of the wrong goal. We have seen people who don't value the importance of loyalty, who will promote undependable, non-team players because they display a particular outstanding individual talent—all in the hope that becoming a manager will elevate their view. It won't.

> Surround yourself with people whose inner values are in sync with yours. The people who surround you are the biggest evangelists of your mission.

Judge the person starting with their loyalty. Surround yourself with people whose inner values are in sync with yours. The people who surround you are the biggest evangelists of your mission.

However, be careful not to confuse disagreement with disloyalty. True loyalists also feel the freedom to speak up, disagree with the boss and others, but build dialogue and discussion on important topics.

LESSON 99
Firing—Doing What Is Right

This is the worst part of the job, yet it is a necessary part of any manager's responsibility. Isn't it hard to find just the perfect staffing level, talent, and knowledge and have that in place in every position?

Compound that with continual growth, and you are always a little too overstaffed (too anticipatory) or too short staffed (not enough foresight).

Needing to "free someone's future" is never easy, but it is usually beneficial to all in the long term. We hate cutting tree branches, but the tree overall grows stronger when you prune. And so it is with the office and business.

No one should be surprised when we have to make a change. The very first person Dr. Jeff ever fired fainted on him in his office. She wasn't falling for him—she was just falling! We try to be as open as we can along the way while a person is with us. They and we know if it's not working out as well or if they are starting to stick out (in a bad way).

We follow all of the labor laws, give oral and written warnings, and the like. Yet there are situations when it's just time for a change— you both know it, and you're both fighting it. We fight because we don't want to fire somebody. They fight because they don't want to lose their job. Someone wrote once that the time managers have the most angst and uneasiness is when they know they need to fire someone.

Afterward, we are relieved and unencumbered by the drag of a person who wasn't with the program, keeping pace, fitting in, whatever.

And what about always waiting until a problem reaches the nth degree, so you'll never lose a case with the state labor board and never make your unemployment workman's comp payment go up? We say hogwash! When you are running a business, you have to make many decisions. Focus on doing what's right for the business, treat people fairly, and you'll be better off. There are consequences with every decision, and if you don't follow the right decision with action, then the consequences may be a little greater. Every medicine we prescribe has therapeutic benefits and side effects. When it's time to fire someone—despite all of our best intentions to train, to guide a person—then we and the person have to take our medicine. We're Rx-ing for a successful business first and foremost.

LESSON 100
Rehiring Previous Employees

It's a pretty simple philosophy: if you leave us, you won't be coming back. In most cases—though there are rare exceptions—rehiring is a mistake. If somebody leaves and then wants to return to our practice, our answer is no. What does it take to convince us? Usually you won't. In the rare case that other managers plead with us to consider it, we really must understand what the person did while they were here the first time, how they interacted with the other people on staff, and why they left. At that point, we think it's important that the person prove themselves and reconvince us that their motives for leaving the first time aren't going to resurface. Keep in mind that if you let someone leave and come back willingly, what kind of message does that send to the rest of your staff? Those people still on staff and their perceptions are my priority.

Someone who left because their husband or wife was transferred is different than someone who left to work locally for more money. The former would often be welcomed back, if they had a great record.

Why do we take a pretty harsh stance on this? It's simple. The people who are with us and stay on staff are *committed*, and we believe in spending our time *on them*. We look for ways that they can improve themselves and the practice together. If there is another opportunity, we want to help them evaluate it. We won't stand in the way of people trying to better themselves. Often, we help existing staff evaluate all the factors, including those beyond just pay, when comparing one job to another. When they do, they often stay. If they choose to leave, it is usually for better reasons than "a nickel more per hour."

Although we continue to try to make our practice the best darn place to work (which includes the money, training, environment, pride of contribution, etc.), some people *are* going to find better positions for themselves at other places. Ugh! It hurts us to have to say that, but it's really true. We're very supportive of those people and their pursuits. We just don't rehire them. That doesn't mean someone can't make a mistake and leave the practice to then learn from their mistake how good they had it and want to come back. That's happened before, and it probably will again. However, in our thirty-plus years of leading practices, we have allowed, perhaps, three people to return. Three times—out of hiring and employing over one thousand people and having hundreds leave for various reasons over thirty years.

Have we been burned by having this type of rehiring philosophy? Perhaps. But we think we have a pretty loyal and committed existing staff who all know that we are committed to them.

LESSON 101
We've Got Your Back

The title of this lesson might make you think this has something to do with chiropractors, and our staff might think it has something to do with our staff Fun Days, when we bring in massage therapists to work on and relax our staff members during the day (a pretty frequent and much appreciated staff benefit). But what we're referring to is that, yes, we expect a high degree of humility, caring, understanding, patience, professionalism, and courtesy out of our staff. We expect them to bend over backward for patients and their needs. But there *are* limits, and if a patient exceeds that limit or takes advantage of our well-meaning staff or doctors, we will step in. And the staff needs to know that we've got their back.

Service does not mean that the patient is always right. You do treat them as though they are right. You offer alternatives. You ameliorate any frustrations. You explain any misperceptions. You start with Recovery efforts in a genuine way and assume we should have done better.

However, swearing at, embarrassing, or personally attacking any of our team members will get a patient kicked out of our office immediately, if we see it happen. Make any of them feel uncomfortable from a physical safety or sexual safety standpoint, or say anything that makes them feel uncomfortable in either of those ways, and we will step in, talk to you, and likely bounce you from the office—or the practice, if you happen to be a staff member harassing another staff member.

Life is way too short, and we are proud of our staff. We will protect and support them above all else. We will be nice to the transgressor, if we must, but if the staff member says they feel uncomfortable, then we will not hesitate to support them. We have their backs, and they must know this. No one would bend over backward for us and for our patients if they were afraid of there being no limits. So we set limits. Patient care is a two-way street and demands respect from both sides.

LESSON 102
The Best They'll Ever Be

People are seldom better than the way they represent themselves on paper. Want to make your job 50 percent easier? If you're hiring a marketing or public relations director or coordinator for your practice, eliminate anybody who does not take enough time to care about the quality of appearance for their cover letter or resume. We have reviewed many resumes of candidates for these types of positions who for some reason chose to represent themselves with a scanned resume copy that is tilted or, worst of all, includes misspellings. In the past, these were candidates who used Xerox copy paper with a dot matrix printer. Guess what? We have never had one of these well-credentialed, poor-appearing candidates turn out to have the requisite attention to detail that is so vital in all areas of our practice—and particularly in marketing and PR. Our advice: eliminate those resumes from consideration *immediately*. As much as you may want to rationalize that this person could be a good candidate when you get to meet them, save yourself the time, hassle, and frustration of hiring somebody who is going to represent you the way they represent themselves—poorly.

LESSON 103
Don't Be a Jerk, or, How Do They Handle Being Served Cold Soup?

When at a restaurant, expect good service, but don't be rude when asking for it. Show some class and adopt the same management philosophy that should hold true within your office: praise in public but criticize in private. Make sure to tip well and let the management know about their employees who provide exceptionally friendly and courteous service. This is another way for your business to put its best foot forward.

We make it a point to take the doctors or key staff we are considering hiring to eat at a restaurant. We like to see how they handle themselves in public. Not just are they refined (or a slob—well that too). More importantly, how do they handle themselves with other people, including the wait staff? Are they polite? Do they demonstrate good manners? How do they handle a misstep in service? This is someone who is going to represent your business, so you need to know how they present themselves in public.

We learn a lot about a potential candidate who is gracious, politely returning a cold soup, versus the person who acts indignant and loudly complains when sending back his soup. You know what we're talking about, and you've witnessed this type of embarrassing behavior. A rude person is not going to be hired, because they would be reflecting us in public, and it is important to us that our doctors and staff reflect us well.

We've often thought it would be smart to intentionally plan a meal mishap, just so we could see how someone responds. If we're with you at lunch and your soup is cold, did the restaurant mess up, or did we plan to have that happen? Either way, handle it with grace and respect.

LESSON 104
The Kegarise Theory of Relativity on Hiring

We frequently make comparisons between our expanding universe and our growing businesses. Einstein proposed a theory on the effects of general relativity and the concept of space-time. We propose the Kegarise Theory of Relativity on Hiring and the corollary: "Should we hire a relative this time?" DON'T!

Have we hired or allowed relatives to be hired within our business? Yes. Has it occasionally worked out to be a good decision? A few times, yes. More often than not, however, despite well-meaning couples, mothers and daughters, fathers and sons, and cousins claiming that they can and will remain professional and not let the relationship interfere in the workplace, it usually does anyway.

They are not lying, nor are they bad people. We're convinced most really do try to draw the line between each other's jobs. However, we all know that, inevitably in the course of business, a reprimand to one is met with a protectionist and sometimes bitter reaction from the other relative.

We, of course, do not allow direct supervisory relationships among relatives, and when you think about it, doesn't that potentially lead to stunting one of the people's professional growth? Despite someone really wanting to take on a particular role in the business, they can't because they'd be working for their relative.

If you do break this suggested guideline in hiring, we caution the manager suggesting it that the person it's going to be toughest on is *THEM*! If they reprimand one relative, they might hear from the other one. If they choose to fire one of the two relatives, there's a fifty-fifty chance they'll receive the other's resignation, sooner or later, too. It's probably unreasonable to not expect emotions to boil over—either directly with the manager (bad enough, but preferred) or via negative gossip or talk with other staff (really not preferred).

Take it from us—leave relativity to Einstein and the cosmologists.

LESSON 105
Sleeping with the Owner

Despite our feelings on the Kegarise Theory of Relativity on Hiring, there is one exception. We own the business! So we may not have hired each other or considered firing each other, but we *do* work together, and we *are* related. Dr. Jeff likes to kid the staff, saying, "I never say categorically *no* to hiring relatives. How could I? I sleep with the owner!"

Married couples in business together face a unique stress. Can you separate the roles you play at home from the roles you must maintain in business? For us, in addition to loving our roles as clinicians, Dr. Susan has historically played the role of CFO, managing banking relationships, accounts, expenses, and accounts payable, while Dr. Jeff has maintained more of a strategic, marketing, visionary role. He has more involvement in overall operations too, although she is the best at cutting through clutter and knowing what needs to change NOW!—particularly in patient flow and optical management.

Business couples need to show a unified strategic front—even more so than nonmarried owners. We both need to sometimes patiently say to staff members, "Let me bounce that off the other owner," before immediately implementing. There will be differences of opinion, and that's okay. Yet it's important that the staff doesn't misperceive two different opinions as strife in the marital relationship. Similarly, each party has to understand that, at work, we play vital roles in the leadership and management of the company. Almost all the time, we see eye to eye (optometry pun intended), but occasionally we don't. In those cases, one of us has to defer or convince the other, depending on the appropriate role and responsibility.

And then we have to go home and perhaps hash it out or discuss the decision process again, somehow separating disagreements at work from disagreements in home life. That's the way it is when you sleep with the owner. Tough as it can be, we wouldn't want to manage the business with anyone else!

LESSON 106
Never Be Completely Satisfied

Perhaps a better title for this section would be "Never Be Complacent." You really *should* be satisfied. Good people who want to improve are always going to challenge themselves to be better. But you should never lull yourself into believing you're doing everything you can in the best way it can be done. This will kill you. You have to have a certain amount of insecurity; that way, you will always get better. There's always someone trying to show that you're not as good as you could be, but there has to be a sense of reasonableness about this. That's why we say it's probably okay to be satisfied, sometimes.

> Good people who want to improve are always going to challenge themselves to be better. But you should never lull yourself into believing you're doing everything you can in the best way it can be done.

Once in a while, you've got to take a step back and say, "Hey, we're doing some good things, and I like the way this is going." But you can't just trick yourself into believing that just because you've found the best way for your practice to do it, there isn't someone out there finding a better way to do it—possibly a new way that your customers or patients are going to appreciate even more than what you do. If you can't find the thrill of the kill in constant improvements, you're in the wrong hunt.

We like competitive people. We enjoy hiring people who have been in competitive sports. They have learned to work together as a team, and something drives them to appreciate not only the success but the efforts that are required in planning, training, and practicing, which are so critical to winning in anything. They usually also share a sense of frustration when a competitor is doing a better job. That should be motivating to all of us. You know these people. They're the ones who generally have a strong sense of pride in what they are doing. They may even have a little bit of an attitude about the competition, one that says, "You're not about to do it better than us!"

Healthy competition is good, and a competitive spirit is great. Look for these people in the hiring process. You'll spend far more time helping refine their behaviors and congratulating them on successes than you will trying to find the right way to motivate them—they were born motivated!

I was greeted in a friendly and cheerful, yet professional, manner.

Outstanding in every respect.

Great experience! Didn't need glasses and they didn't push me to purchase them.

I love this place! I loved it before now when I was the patient, but I love it even more after I took my daughter there and saw how sweet they treated her.

Consummate professionals!

Everyone seemed so happy!

CHAPTER 6

Focus on Systems that Provide Better Service to Patients

> *Every system is perfectly designed to yield the results that it gets.*
>
> **—Dr. Paul Batalden**

I n past academic health professional training programs, doctors were taught a "your" patient approach. It is *your* patient so *you* run the test, *you* evaluate the result, *you* read the scan, *you* repeat if necessary. This led to a very technically viewed approach to patient care. *I* do this; *I* do that; it's *my* patient, my care, my practice.

The fallacies that are inherent with this approach are obvious. First, it ignores the reality that the majority of the time, a patient interacts with a physician office's staff and not the doctor. Scheduling an appointment and inquiring about insurance coverage, billing statements, and medication refills are but a few common examples of nondoctor interactions in patient care.

Second, to the extent that all care is "I" (by the doctor), the care team is relegated to more menial tasks, those too unimportant for the doctor to handle. This leads to less happiness, engagement, and development of employees. Over time, it is common for doctors and offices with this mentality to possess lower-paid, less-ambitious, shorter-term employees. Most simply realize they can't grow and become self-fulfilled to the level of their capabilities. Some may move on to other opportunities. Doctors then become frustrated with high turnover and start to believe that, "You just can't find and keep good staff. No one is loyal anymore." We often see many of these doctors surrender human resource management because it is too hard and unfulfilling, possibly blaming the staff for doctor woes, when the root cause of the problem is the doctors' managerial outlook.

Progressive doctors now look at healthcare as provided by a care team. The ideal "we" do this and "we" do that, "our" care is provided when each participant functions to a higher level and supports the doctor, who should be focused on teaching others how to respond to patients. This requires new and time-consuming management focus, skills, and energy. Indeed, one of the biggest stress points for doctors is when they are forced, often due to their own success, to move from an "I care" system to a "we care" philosophy. We call this needing to "grow past themselves."

The sooner the doctor and team start to think and approach care as a process-based system, the better and faster they will grow capable of serving more people and the more consistent will be the care provided. Systems require communication, understanding, alignment, monitoring, measurement—all more complex management tasks that seem to cut into a patient-care focus. Many doctors begrudge this responsibility and fight it or surrender it to others to deal with. Yet much like a differential diagnostic process in patient care, learning to develop, incorporate, deploy, and monitor systems to help patients can be just as rewarding. Want to improve the care and patient experience for more people you serve? Develop, implement, and train a systems-based approach to care.

LESSON 107
Loyalty Matrix

Dr. Jeff attended a meeting on microsystems as faculty and participant at Dartmouth College and was fortunate to meet and discuss service with Horst Schulze, past chairman of the board of Ritz-Carlton. Who better to model service philosophies from than a person who led his company to winning the Malcolm Baldrige National Quality Award?

Mr. Schulze stressed *saying hello well*, *meeting expectations*, and *saying goodbye well* to be critical to good in-service delivery. He also said that in meeting expectations, customers want timeliness, zero defects, and quality service, and of those three, service was the most valued and important.

We have always said hello well and continually stress this with our team. We say goodbye well yet could do it even better. We'll be working on making that memorable. We have looked deeply into the *meet expectations* component. Schulze said don't screw up, be on time, and care more (our extrapolation of his words.) We believe in this so much that, combined with the many touch points and data that we track on patients, we have condensed a vital few into our "loyalty grid." We review this grid and its indicators as a part of our monthly loyalty review.

We've massaged his service matrix into our own, stressing all of what he mentioned but then breaking it down further into key measurables for each of the main areas of the eye-care practice, front desk and administrative, and clinical and optical.

Loyalty Matrix

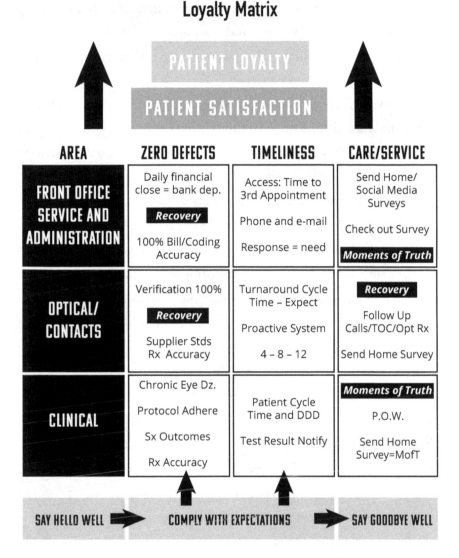

AREA	ZERO DEFECTS	TIMELINESS	CARE/SERVICE
FRONT OFFICE SERVICE AND ADMINISTRATION	Daily financial close = bank dep. *Recovery* 100% Bill/Coding Accuracy	Access: Time to 3rd Appointment Phone and e-mail Response = need	Send Home/ Social Media Surveys Check out Survey *Moments of Truth*
OPTICAL/ CONTACTS	Verification 100% *Recovery* Supplier Stds Rx Accuracy	Turnaround Cycle Time – Expect Proactive System 4 – 8 – 12	*Recovery* Follow Up Calls/TOC/Opt Rx Send Home Survey
CLINICAL	Chronic Eye Dz. Protocol Adhere Sx Outcomes Rx Accuracy	Patient Cycle Time and DDD Test Result Notify	*Moments of Truth* P.O.W. Send Home Survey=MofT

SAY HELLO WELL → COMPLY WITH EXPECTATIONS → SAY GOODBYE WELL

We genuinely believe that satisfying patients is not enough. Exciting them, surprising them, delighting them, making them raving fans—many excellent books have supplied their own adjectives for the customer (patient) who is so wowed that they not only return but recommend the office to others.

Our goal is not to satisfy but to delight. Our mission is to create loyalty in our patients. We build more than a transactional relationship. We inexorably create generative, growing, and strengthening relationships between patients and doctors.

Now, we're realistic. We cannot or won't wow everybody! But we *will* try.

However, on the path to wowing them and creating loyalists is the foundational step of satisfying them. Only once satisfied with basic service needs and expectations will we have a chance to wow them up to the loyalist level.

We stress that, because these areas are so important to us, we *must* have data. Further, we must understand the trends and what the data are telling us in these most critical areas. This is an important component to measuring and monitoring for managers.

First, managers need to make sure the process for gathering data is solid and reproducible. There has to be integrity in the numbers reviewed. Second, one has to understand what the goals are for each process indicator and continuously work to improve the performance. Third, if all the indicators are tracked and trended and performance seems good, then managers, doctors, and staff must realize that this is only an "ante up." It is just a beginning, because we have likely "satisfied" a lot of people. Satisfied people do *not* recommend us to their friends—wowed people do. On the NPS (or net promoter score) findings, they are the "neutrals." Yet they are important because satisfied people have the potential for us to wow them. That could make them loyalists. And that is the goal!

LESSON 108
Treat the Person First, Then the Process—Recovery

Errors and unmet needs occur in any service industry. In healthcare, and particularly eye care, we are no different. Like head football coach Nick Saban of the University of Alabama said, "We have a process." Our process, called the Caring Alert Recovery System—Recovery, for short—is designed to handle these unmet patient expectations. We teach and try to model the Recovery process at all times. We listen well and try to ascertain what the patient is saying, wants, and needs. Then we follow the Recovery process. And, as Coach Saban would say, "Trust the process."

Too many service organizations do not pay attention to their errors or times when the delivery of service does not match the patient's expectations. We find that most of the time when we screw up, it was a process error, not a personal error. Even if it *was* a person, we *are* human. No one gets terminated at our office for trying to help patients and doing their job—even if they occasionally mess up.

> We find that most of the time when we screw up, it was a process error, not a personal error. Even if it *was* a person, we *are* human.

Also important is documenting the event, and we train everyone in Recovery behaviors with patients. This is so often overlooked in general business and particularly in healthcare. As though no one wants to fess up and say, "I am sorry; we should have done better." We train our staff to use three Recovery steps (and sometimes five) as follows:

1. Apologize: Make it personal.

2. Sense of urgency: Show it is important.

3. Empathize: Treat the patient, then the problem.

4. Symbolic expression: Make it up to them.

5. Follow up: It still matters, and we want to be sure you know.

Why three and possibly five? The first three should be routine for any frustration, complaint, or mistake we make. The very first determination we make is whether the patient is annoyed or victimized. If someone is annoyed, the first three steps will neutralize and not exacerbate the situation (or exasperate the patient).

Only when someone is victimized (based on what they tell us or how they feel), do we need to try to make it right with some monetary fix. Truthfully, we occasionally will do the same at the staff's discretion with annoyed patients, but that decision is made on a case-by-case basis.

Our goal is always to follow up. It shows that we genuinely care and are sorry and adds to the patient's understanding that we aren't perfect, but we do try to be, and we aren't afraid to admit a mistake and make it right.

The Caring Alert form is used to document and show the steps our staff takes in Recovery.

The staff member directly involved in the Recovery effort is responsible for filling it out and placing their initials next to the steps they have completed.

Quality Caring Alert

Please put in Office Manager's Inbox

Person(s) Affected: _____ Date: _____

Address/Phone Number: _____

Referring Physician: _____

Is person Annoyed/Victimized?   **A**   **V**

Reason: _____

_____

_____

_____

_____

_____

Initials

A&V

_____ Apology

_____ Sense of Urgency

_____ Empathy

V

_____ Symbolic Expression

_____ Follow up

RECOVERY STEPS TAKEN

Make it Personal

Show the problem is important to us

Treat the patient ... then the problem

How we want to make it up to them

Phone call or note

Quality Caring Alert

Please put in Office Manager's Inbox

Person(s) Affected: **Britney Spears**   Date: **05/07/2018**

Address/Phone Number: **123 Main Street, Franklin, TN 37067**
615-123-4567

Referring Physician: **Dr. Jones**

Is person Annoyed/Victimized?   A   (V) **Victimized**

Reason: **Patient came in today under the impression they had an exam with JLK. Not on the schedule and had rescheduled multiple meetings to be here. See my OM notes for more info.**

Initials	RECOVERY STEPS TAKEN
A&V	
__KJ__ Apology	Make it Personal
__KJ__ Sense of Urgency	Show the problem is important to us
__KJ__ Empathy	Treat the patient ... then the problem
V	
_____ Symbolic Expression	How we want to make it up to them
_____ Follow up	Phone call or note

We first saw this described in concept in Ron Zemke's *The Service Edge: 101 Companies that Profit from Customer Care*. We've massaged and modified it over time yet have used it as part of our loyalty-building systems—in healthcare practices large and small.

LESSON 109
Pareto-izing Our Recovery Results

We categorize the reason or reasons for each Caring Alert. For instance, if a contact lens order was delayed, and we forgot to tell the patient of the delay, we may categorize the reasons as "contact lens order delay" and "communication failure."

Using the Pareto principle, we then try to note where errors are occurring most and dig down to remedy the processes. We have only a certain amount of time, and therefore, using our limited time resources wisely, we should concentrate on solving frequently recurring errors (known as the vital few). Our review of the Caring Alert data comes both monthly, when we see the individual Caring Alert sheets, and every six months, when a Pareto chart, such as the one shown below, is produced.

Caring Alert Summary Sample

PARETO DIAGRAM

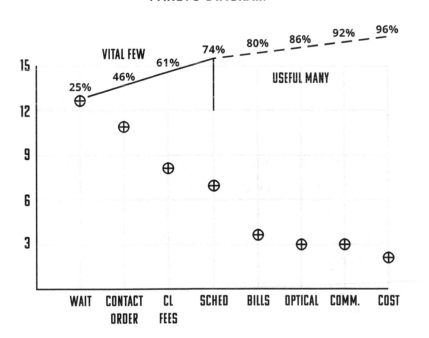

LESSON 110
You May Not Be an Owner, Yet You Still Own

"Dropped the ball," "fell through the cracks," "slipped my mind"—each of these common expressions may be heard when a person fails to hand off a patient or staff message effectively. In the case of Caring Alerts and service Recovery, a mistake could cause a small problem to become a bigger and harder-to-handle issue.

Anyone on staff may be the recipient of a patient's frustration. It could be on the phone, in person, by text, or by email. That staff member may or may not have been involved in the care or know any of the details of the care situation. Yet they received the feedback, so they own it.

Each individual represents the whole team. Therefore, they own the Recovery response until the issue has been satisfactorily resolved and the patient neutralized. If they need to get another team member involved, then they do not do the following:

- Leave a voice mail for that person assuming it will be heard

- Delegate to the office manager or assume someone else will handle it

- Leave a sticky note on an already cluttered staff member's work area

Owning it means solving it or effectively recovering as trained and getting others involved as needed. It is never disowned until another staff member says, "I will handle this and own it from here." The initial recipient then fills out the Caring Alert and initializes the steps in Recovery administered before giving it to the next person (who now owns the resolution).

Fortunately, Recovery is relatively rare. Yet as we ratchet up our expectations, so do patients. Caring alerts may represent less than 0.5 percent of visits to our clinics, but each staff member who owns one has a chance to cure. Recovery "cures" are an essential part of attentive patient service.

LESSON 111
Monthly Loyalty Review

It is one thing to have beliefs and methods of interactive service. It is another to train, reinforce, and review. The deciding vote about how well we are acting in concert with our prescribed behaviors and goals lies with our patients. Where are we strong, and where do we need to improve?

As we see patients, we do get a gut feeling in our "abdominal computers" about how we're doing. More WOWs from happy patients—as opposed to "Do you know that this happened to me in your office" stories—suggests that people are being well cared for.

"In God we trust; all others must show data" is a quote famously repeated by President Ronald Reagan. Same here. Most of the care in your office is being provided by other people. Unless you are a doctor who does everything in your office, from greeting patients to shepherding them through the entire office process, insurance claims and all, your part of the patient interaction is a relatively small portion of the total contact that patients have with your office. That's why you need to establish behavioral norms and expectations for each department and follow up by assuring, *through data*, that each and every department's service indicators are being achieved.

We review service indicators for one hour minimum every month in what we term a Monthly Loyalty Review. We follow up patient complaints with questions and even send personal notes to some patients to make sure we solved their problems or to make sure they know that we are paying attention to their comments. We think it also helps that team leaders and those responsible for the data tracking know that we are paying attention too!

Here is a sample Monthly Loyalty Review form:

MONTHLY LOYALTY REVIEW

Due the fifth of each month in Monthly Operations Report
* Apple Send-Home Surveys—graphs of results

Marketing and administrator in charge of surveys, given every other month.
* Caring Alerts

Front-line staff handles, gives CA summary to Hannah, Hannah reviews and follows up, Hannah categorizes with Dr. Keg and reviews monthly, every six months Pareto-ized summary for review, six-month and one-year trend analyses.
* Focus group need and opportunities

* Loyalty Matrix

Dr. Keg reviews data in each category monthly and quarterly.
* NPS number and graph for each office

Office manager reports
* BirdEye surveys and comments for each office Marketing coordinator summary review

* Online and social media scores and review of interaction numbers

Yelp, Google, Facebook, Instagram, Twitter, Pinterest, LinkedIn, and YouTube?

Who are they looking for and what are they saying?

LESSON 112
Communication Marketing—
Listen, Document, Target

Marketing has a lot of components to it. Advertising, public relations, education, merchandising, postsale reinforcement, and many others. We don't do a lot of advertising. There is a time and place for it, and it may work for some offices, but for most of *our* relationship needs, advertising is not target focused enough to help us build individual relationships.

Relationship building starts with good listening. It is enhanced by good documentation (which allows institutional memory) and is further supplemented by targeted communication. When it comes to communication, books have been written on mass customization, and the digital age has been replete with Amazon-like algorithms designed to proactively suggest and regularly remind consumers about purchase options.

We're no Amazon. We are a mom-and-pop optometry business (literally!). So how do we use technology and enhance relationships? Through good and frequent communication targeted to our patients' needs and wants. Often, they have expressed those needs and wants, while at other times we have to anticipate, recommend, or make them aware.

Above all, we want to be known for providing the most up-to-date eye health and vision information. Yet we don't want to spam or harass people. Here is what we are currently doing, which seems to strike a good balance:

Clinical blogs—This is for the most current information. It's timely, educational, and actionable. We usually do these one to two times per month.

Patient newsletter—Newsletters—occasionally in print but usually six to ten times per year through email blasts—highlight our new people and new services available at the office. We like to write in a style that stresses involvement of the patient with our office and doctors and staff.

Registry nurturing—Once a patient has a diagnosis, expresses an interest, mentions a hobby, or seems particularly interested in a conversational topic, we make it a point to put them on a clinical or topical registry. We then set a schedule to update the patients on the registry on a regular or as-needed basis. If you are a fisherman, we may update you on the most recent fishing glasses and lens technology to reduce glare off the water. This might be one time per year. If you have been diagnosed or have a loved one with macular degeneration, we are more likely going to communicate with you as a part of the macular degeneration registry two to three times per year. Over time, we want patients to know about the disease, what tests we do, why, what they can do to help prevent problems, and what treatments we have available.

Kindness permeates all through the staff.

I appreciate feeling valued.

Can't recommend this clinic highly enough, especially for anyone whose prescription isn't straightforward vision correction.

CHAPTER 7
Focus on Efficiency and Effectiveness

*It's better to go slow in the right direction
than to go fast in the wrong direction.*

—Simon Sinek

W e have all heard the prevailing mantra, "To deliver healthcare today, doctors have to see more patients in less time." Poor access and long waits have become standard expectations for patients and doctors alike. *It does not have to be that way.*

With a focus on access to care, information, appointments, and education, balanced by doctor-team interaction and

> Poor access and long waits have become standard expectations for patients and doctors alike. *It does not have to be that way.*

a value-driven process, modeled after non-healthcare-effective flow systems, the status quo of doctor visit equals unnecessary wait can be changed.

We never promote just going faster. Some doctors will still beat their chests by bragging about the number of patients they saw in an afternoon. That is a system built to satisfy the doctor. It is like a badge of honor for some. What you don't hear them discuss is how the patient viewed the experience. That needs to be a part of the equation.

We also do not advocate or subscribe to the mistaken conclusion that "the more time a doctor spends, the more the patient appreciates the visit." There are practicalities at play, and research has not shown a correlation between more doctor time and the quality of the patient-care experience.

We advocate "effective" care. Care should be judged by efficiency, through reducing the patient's non-value-added time, improving the patient experience, and always measuring value in relation to the patient—a system built for the patient and measured for success on their terms.

$$\textbf{V effect} = \frac{\textbf{PtSat}_{(NPS)}}{\textbf{E (time)}}$$

For example, if a doctor sees more patients, yet surveys show lower care experience scores (as judged by patients), then it is efficient, yes, effective, no.

In contrast, what if a doctor sees more patients; provides more care, better access, education, and information; and achieves a reduction of patient total cycle time in office, with improvements in the patient satisfaction and loyalty score? Now that's effective.

Access to care is so important that we often adjust the equation to account for it when measuring success for a population of patients.

$$V \text{ effect} = \frac{PtSat_{(NPS)}}{E \text{ (time)}} \times \frac{1}{Access^*}$$

*(time to the third available appointment day)

This seems to better address the patient's dual needs of ability to get in and ability to experience an effective, value-assessed visit by spending as little non-value-added time in the office as possible. Neither doctors nor patients like to be rushed through an impersonal system. Neither, however, is tolerant of inefficiencies, duplication, and waste—what the Japanese call *muda*.

Strive for effectiveness, Doctor, yet don't be fooled. Don't just focus on the care provided and ignore the care deferred. Your care is not better because you do it all. Your patients will embrace and trust your care-built team when it performs well in getting them in, seeing them efficiently, and providing them respect and all the things they want and need. That is producing value, and we should all expect that in our visits to the doctor.

LESSON 113
If Your Reception Room Becomes a Waiting Room, That's Inventory

When you really think about it, efficient and effective patient flow through our offices is a complex system made up of smaller, much simpler subsystems. Though ours is very personalized, it includes many of the same elements of a complex manufacturing system. Whenever you have backlog because of inefficiency, you tend to have increased inventory. In a medical practice, the patients are the "inventory." You must consider this as you evaluate patient flow. Ideally, if you can develop your office facility design to have "holding areas" in front of each process (front office check-in, technical workup, dilating, surgical counseling, special testing, etc.), you can clearly reveal the bottlenecks in patient flow. The bottlenecks are usually where you see the increasing inventory of patients.

When you start to develop a waiting time problem, look for the bottlenecks first. Understand that those bottlenecks will limit your capacity for patient flow and that any inefficiency in those areas will be passed downstream in the system. The doctor's ability to see a patient efficiently is limited by the ability of your office to see patients efficiently through these bottleneck areas. This doesn't just come from practical experience; it is borne out by statistical and theoretical models. To solve patient waiting time problems, divert resources to aid patient flow through your bottleneck areas (see lesson 115, "The Doctor Should Be Your Constraint").

LESSON 114
Don't Balance Capacity with Patient Demand

Wouldn't it make sense to match the demand of patients with the capacity of the doctor? Intuitively, that makes sense. If five patients want to see a doctor in a given hour, and that doctor can see five patients per hour for their capacity, it should be perfect, right?

Unfortunately, it doesn't work that way.

Variability comes into play. Patients arrive late, some need more care, and some need less. Inevitably, someone has to use the bathroom, the doctor gets called away, or something else goes wrong along the way.

Never try to balance a doctor's patient capacity to make it *equal* to patient demand. The more you accomplish this stable equilibrium, the more inefficient your system will be—and the closer you will be to bankruptcy! Make sure your capacity slightly exceeds your patient demand. Patient flow and patient satisfaction will improve dramatically, while total patient time in the office and waiting time will decrease.

We try to schedule at 80 percent of a predicted (or actual) doctor's capacity. If, in the current system flow, a doctor's capacity is five patients per hour, then we'd like to schedule that doctor with four patients per hour. If we change the system and reduce the number of extra things a doctor needs to do, and their capacity increases to six patients per hour, then we try to schedule at 80 percent of six, which is 4.8—or five patients per hour.

The more accurate and realistic we are about capacity, the happier the doctors and patients are, and the better the day goes.

LESSON 115
The Doctor Should Be Your Constraint

The classic business book *The Goal* by Eliyahu Goldratt incorporated the "Theory of Constraints" into modern manufacturing processes. How does this relate to eye care? Goldratt's theory addresses the following:

- Looking at patient flow overall

- Identifying steps and timing throughout each process

- Minimizing bottlenecks to improve flow throughput

First, make the doctor the limiting factor. Second, reduce the demands on the constraint (the doctor) to allow for more capacity. This is one of the reasons we need to know any given doctor's capacity for seeing patients and provide them with a work-up tech (or two) and a scribe.

In optometry, a refracting tech, special testing tech, and contact lens tech added to the system will improve flow and add to a doctor's capacity to see patients.

LESSON 116
Active, Not Passive, Systems

Active and passive systems are analogous in some ways to pull versus push systems. How do we accomplish active notification systems in the office rather than passive care? Here are a few ways:

1. We call or email or text patients as soon as we hear there is going to be a back order or delay on their product being delivered.

2. We communicate to patients if the product packaging on their contact lenses will look different and tell them when and why any changes are being made to a product they already love.

3. We tell patients in advance—not when they arrive at the office—if there is a change to the doctor they might be seeing due to sickness or schedule changes.

4. If this change of doctors is so sudden that we don't have time to use the active notification system, then we do the next best thing. We type up a quick patient update regarding their care in the office that day. These let patients know if there is a doctor change, if there are deficiencies in equipment that day that will prevent something from happening, or if there is anything they might notice as different. Everyone likes a heads-up about change, and our patients appreciate this.

5. We text or call patients before they arrive if a doctor is running late because of an unforeseen patient emergency or a capacity issue.

6. We notify patients that a product we have been waiting for

is finally available and may benefit them. Using registries is one way we are prepared to employ active systems of care.

7. We always enter patients' communication preferences in our system. Do they prefer to receive a text? An email to a work address? We notify patients in the manner they prefer. And active database updates are a part of the active systems we employ, so we keep those preferences current.

8. As we described earlier, we try to greet patients at the door by name, before they need to identify themselves.

9. Technicians know they have patients to work up, so they don't wait at the back for the front office to notify them of a patient being ready. The techs go out and help greet and check in the patient.

10. If we are responding to frequent calls from our patients on a certain subject, we take this opportunity to educate or inform them *actively* on that subject.

11. We notify patients when they check in if their doctor is running behind so they can plan accordingly and so we've shaped their expectations.

12. We offer patients the opportunity to upgrade their appointments and minimize any waits and delays.

What other ways can you use active rather than passive systems to provide better care? It's worth thinking about.

LESSON 117
Top Gun—Scribe as Wingman

The institution of electronic medical records is a huge step in the direction of better and more consistent patient care. We know this. Doctors' notes being legible should make chart review easier, reduce medical errors from illegibility, and reduce duplication of testing. But are they more efficient? As my former boss, Tom Lewis, used to say, "Do you want the short answer, no, or the long answer, nooooooooooooo?"

In keeping with the concept of the doctor as constraint, to be efficient, doctors need to concentrate on patient care, and scribes in the room need to concentrate on assisting and charting. There are books and courses written on what it means to be a good scribe. Heck, *we* have a full training module on it for our staff. Yet sometimes we find a good metaphor is more effective than all the training manuals we write. We tell scribes that they are the doctor's "wingman." And, as Jester told Maverick in *Top Gun*, "You never, never leave your wingman!"

This means that the scribe should ideally be with the doctor for all parts of the examination. But what happens when the scribe has to finish up with a patient as the doctor moves to the next room, or walk a patient to the front office, or do a quick additional test? Those are patient flow decisions that doctors and their scribes need to keep in mind and decide together.

If, in a given situation, the scribe must do something other than stay with the doctor, then the scribe should remember about being a wingman and, after completing the task, get back with the doctor pronto. Do whatever it takes to complete your task, but don't get caught up in any unnecessary conversation or delay. The doctor as pilot needs their wingman!

LESSON 118
More Calls Out Than In

If we are doing our jobs and are active and not passive, we should have more phone calls going out than coming in. That's because we always call, text, and email to alert patients that their glasses or contact lenses have been received and are ready for pickup as soon as we receive them.

The goal is that no one calls to say, "When will my glasses be ready?" If they do, that means we did not cement a delivery date at order with the patient. Or that we're late in notifying them—and that's inexcusable. Or that we missed the fact that their glasses were delayed at one of our vendor labs. It's inexcusable for the lab to not notify us and then for us to not notify the patient and set up a new promise date. (That's a hot board item too!)

We can track calls out versus calls in on any given day in each department. If outgoing calls exceed incoming calls, we're being successful in accomplishing our proactive system of service. If incoming calls exceed outgoing calls, it's *muda* and needs to be improved. *Muda* is a quality term the Japanese use to describe waste or unnecessary delay in a system. Our staff is well versed in the concept and will often point out wasted steps in patient flow, paperwork duplication, or other inefficient processes as being *muda*.

Top-notch "cream of the crop" doctors, technicians, and optical and office staff.

I have been a patient in numerous optometrist and ophthalmologist offices in the last ten or twenty years and can say unequivocally that this office is far above any in my experience. The welcoming, friendly attitude, genuine concern, and joy in serving patients was obvious from my first encounter.

Five-star service from the phone call, exam, and check-out. This is a class-act operation.

These people are quite literally the best! I was driving through Nashville on vacation and had forgotten extra contacts in my home state of Illinois. Feeling slightly blind, I popped in to their store thinking I would have to pay for an entire eye exam. No way! They helped me request my current prescription from my eye doctor at home, and then were able to give me contacts without the need for a whole separate eye exam! I can't thank these people enough.

CHAPTER 8

Focus on Creating Consistency in Imaging and Marketing

It is what's inside that counts but what's outside that attracts.

—Author unknown

I t has often been said that what you do is more revealing than what you say, or alternatively, watch what they do, not what they say.

The focus on service and patient relationships as a differentiator should be woven into every process, decision, and strategic innovation pursued. Similarly, the way you as a business look, educate, communicate, and market must enhance, not conflict with, the underlying philosophical focus.

We see this strategic positioning mismatch in healthcare all too frequently. Organizations trying to compete to be all things to all people. The large academic center that goes overboard to try to advertise care and compassion, when, in reality, the endowment and funding as a teaching hospital will always be focused on new equipment, techniques, and innovations. And, further, their leadership stresses research dollar grants for those things, not for enhancing the patient experience.

Often worse is the healthcare practice, business, or organization that does not know what they are nor has a differentiation to stress. They may be diffused in their goals, and their image is likely to be too. For example, the doctor says, "No one cares for patients more than us," yet every sign you see says, "Special Discount," "Big Price Reduction!" or "50 percent off today." This is a focus on price, not customer care.

> Every internal or external image or communication or educational piece reflects your care. Be consistent.

Every internal or external image or communication or educational piece reflects your care. Be consistent. Keep the colors, fonts, and delivery consistent in everything visible or presented to patients. The little things are as important as the big things, as each one shapes an impression and tells a story. Make sure you own that story and that it represents you, your care team, and your care in the way you want to be represented.

LESSON 119
Fonts and Consistency

Much has been written about the psychology of typography. Staying focused and disciplined by using standard fonts, as the authors say in *The 4 Disciplines of Execution*, "Says easy, does hard."

Dr. Jeff is the frequent butt of jokes by our staff regarding his font preferences. For what it's worth, here are his strong opinions about fonts:

- Calibri—Don't like it at all. Why Microsoft Word made this the standard default baffles me.

- Times New Roman—Professional, classic, and used to project that image on clinical, professional correspondence.

- Bookman Old Style—Love the look for teaching and manuals, so we use it for our Tiger Educational Institute.

- Georgia—Friendly, accessible, and often our choice for internal communication, spreadsheets, summaries, and communications.

- Arial—Used to be our favorite—now it's Georgia—but Arial is quicker to find in the alphabetical drop-down list!

Font consistency goes along with using standard Pantone colors and consistent logos. A consistently used font helps to position the writing in the manner you want it absorbed.

LESSON 120
Anything Written Represents Us

It's expensive to use an outside printer to make sure that all educational materials are professionally produced. Where we can—brochures, pamphlets, educational disease topics—we do send out for printing. However, there are many items you can produce yourself that still project a professional appearance because of the advent of high-quality color laser printing.

Everything we hand to patients is a reflection of our quality. More so, it is a reflection of our attention to detail and level of care. Forms, practice demographics, educational information, and any other paper given to patients represents us—so it better be clean, legible, and straight on the page. No smudges or black marks from bad copiers!

Our care is reflected in what patients receive from us. Bad copies reflect bad care. Sharp, good copies reflect our thoughtful care and attention to detail.

LESSON 121
Pet Peeve—Handout Inconsistency

In optometry and medicine, every pharmaceutical, frame, lens, equipment, device, or test manufacturer produces a handout to educate us, the doctors and staff, on their products. They usually also produce patient information handouts that they hope we'll place in our office for patients to read—or they clandestinely place them themselves.

In many physician offices a bevy of these multicolored, variable-sized handouts or pamphlets are displayed (or scattered haphazardly) in the reception room.

We think it looks terribly sloppy, and that is not the image we want to project. Therefore, as mentioned earlier, we write and customize information for patients. These handouts may discuss the basics of a procedure or service: What is it? Who gets it? What to expect from it? And they all match and look professionally congruent. We display them professionally (see photo below) all together with our logo, color, and a consistent appearance.

Overkill or fastidious, you say? Anal retentive, you exclaim? Perhaps, but mostly protective and proud of our image and always working to project it.

LESSON 122
Laminate for Emphasis

When speaking to a group or conference attendees, some things may need to be emphasized more. The key to emphasizing that importance? Laminate it! Isn't it true that you perceive a laminated handout as more important, as something you're meant to keep for a long time?

Want to really reflect importance? Use the extrathick 7 ml lamination to achieve maximum firmness, readability, and appearance of importance.

LESSON 123
Our Practice Logo

Develop a strong, eye-catching practice logo—and maybe a "sublogo" for each of your services areas—and respect the way it's used. Have a style manual that clearly defines three or four ways that your logo and name can be used—and emphasize that it *should not* be used in other ways. This keeps you from having the practice represented in different images, shapes, and forms.

Consistency is key. After a while, you may want to change the logo or the way it's used. But if you've been changing it on every marketing piece you put out, no one will notice when the "new you" arrives.

Enforce the idea that all materials handed out to patients internally or used for marketing or practice identification externally must follow the style manual for font, colors, and appearance.

Logo Names, Fonts, and RGB Color

COMPANY	COLOR VALUES IN RGB			FONT
	R	G	B	
Cool Springs EyeCare and Donelson EyeCare	12	28	140	Times New Roman or Arial
The Tiger Institute	232	117	17	Bookman Old Style
	0	0	0	
Performance Vision Therapy	60	177	229	Arial
	107	107	107	
Doctors Help Doctors	119	45	107	Constantia
	173	175	170	
The Competitive Edge	196	30	58	Leelawadee
	0	136	206	
	0	0	0	
	147	149	152	
CPD	195	212	237	Georgia/ Times New Roman
	0	0	0	
Dry Eye Center	13	116	186	Cambria
	142	199	63	
	107	110	111	

Who We Are: Our Companies

Primary Care Optometry Services, Franklin, Tennessee
(South Nashville, Tennessee)

Primary Care Optometry Services, Donelson, Tennessee
(East Nashville, Tennessee)

Vision Therapy and Traumatic Brain Injury

Leadership and Management Consulting

Dry Eye Specialty Services

LESSON 124
Leave a Business Card

Earlier in our career, a wise optometrist, Dr. Sid Goldstein, told us he always left a business card on the table at a restaurant when he left. It's an inexpensive way of reminding someone of your name, business, and location. Thanks, Sid!

We can't say we *always* do this, but we occasionally do. We especially do it when we encounter a great attitude and friendly, competent service. We've hired some of our best people from restaurant waitstaffs. Perhaps they wanted a change in their hours, a new challenge, or something that could become a profession instead of just a job.

Some of those people are still with us, while others provided valuable services while employed and are now nurses, physicians, optometrists, and physical therapists. We'd like to think we helped pique their interest in healthcare. Most of them perpetuated our hospitality and service reputation, and they got their chance to do that because we already saw their service behaviors in action. You can more easily teach the specific skills if someone already demonstrates the underlying behavior. We are always looking to recruit talented, friendly people.

LESSON 125
Dressing Our Offices

Presenting a consistent, professional, pleasing appearance is another way to reflect your great service. We like offices where the decor flows well and matches the uniform color theme of the staff. Wait—did we just say the walls and the staff should look the same? No. What we did say is that we prefer to not design offices with pleasing colors and ambience and then clash those colors with conflicting colors for staff uniforms. It's a subtle perceptual thing that adds to the patient's comfort. But, then again, we're eye doctors, so perception and color are especially important to us!

> Presenting a consistent, professional, pleasing appearance is another way to reflect your great service.

LESSON 126
It's Cold Outside, Yet We All Dress the Same

Tennessee has a relatively warm climate, yet we do get our share of winter weather. And with air conditioning and everyone on staff having varying internal thermostats, staff may want a jacket on inside the building. We think uniformity reflects well to patients. That's why if a staff member needs another layer of clothing inside, we provide a nice Nike zip-up sport fleece emblazoned with our logo. In addition to a few dress code rules that are aimed at casting a more uniform and professional image, these fleeces look good and keep everyone happy and warm!

Though it may change over time, here is the simple dress code in our office:

- Doctors—Business or business casual with white coats preferred

- Clinical staff and technicians—Scrubs with daily matching colors for everyone

- Front office—Business casual or business

- Optical—Business casual or business (matching colors for special events)

- Administrative—Business casual or business

LESSON 127
Are You Fully Dressed?

When we talk about our staff being appropriately dressed, we're not just talking about technical staff having matching scrub colors for the day. That's important, but there's more to it than that.

In addition to a uniform (if one is required), everyone should have the following items on their person:

- Name tag—How can someone compliment you by name otherwise?

- Business card—To be handed out to build or add to the personalization of care and to reinforce the importance of the team member.

- BBs card—We have them, train on them, and insist on the behaviors—everyone's required to have them.

- Laminated goal card—If it's important enough for us to close all offices and communicate these goals, it's important for employees to have them on their person.

LESSON 128
What's in Your Pocket?

Reinforcing the uniform is hard but not impossible. Here a few of the ways we do it:

1. At a staff meeting, we'll say, "Raise your hand and show your BBs card." You'd be surprised at the number of people who have a great excuse for not having it. "Dr. Keg, I carry it with me regularly, but I just changed purses last night," or "I just left it in my locker—only for the staff meeting, though."

2. In the halls of the clinic, we'll say, "Can you show me your BBs card? Or your goal card?" If they have it, we'll say, "Thanks for being well dressed," or "Here's $10—lunch is on us." If they don't have it? "Remember, it's part of your uniform, so make sure you have it on you from now on."

3. If someone is consistently "not dressed," we'll say something like, "The next time I ask and you don't have it, I'm going to get you one, but I may tape it to your pocket for the rest of the month. That way I and everyone else can see that you're dressed."

No one wants the third option. But you know what? It's important to us that the staff are dressed appropriately. People often avoid pain more than they pursue pleasure. A BBs card displayed outside the pocket wouldn't be pleasurable.

LESSON 129
Develop a Good Relationship with a Nice Restaurant

Get to know the owner, the maître d', and a particular server of a restaurant. Make sure they know your name. Pick a restaurant that is classy but not stuffy. You're going to use this restaurant for key business meetings. Negotiations and relationship building always go better in a comfortable and unthreatening environment. You'll be amazed at the aura of importance and credibility you take on when your dining guest notes the restaurant's familiarity with you personally.

In *Swim with the Sharks without Being Eaten Alive*, Harvey Mackay recommends this technique and even going one step further. Prepay with a credit card at the restaurant. That way, when you are done with the meal and discussion, you can just get up and leave. Talk about an air of importance and personal trust. A little bit of preplanning can help with that.

LESSON 130
My Favorite Restaurant—a Table Full of Notes

While Harvey Mackay gives us a good recommendation for having a favorite restaurant, we have our own specification. What is our favorite kind of restaurant?

Easy—good food, good service, and paper covering the tablecloth! Believe it or not, we have solved a lot of business and patient-care issues writing on paper tablecloths.

Innovations at dinner just seem to blossom! And the best part? You can tear off the part of the paper tablecloth you've written on and take it with you. You ought to see the large scraps of tablecloth we have organized in our files! While strategy can start on a napkin, we prefer a restaurant with a paper tablecloth—it gives us room for bigger ideas.

LESSON 131
I'll Take a Four Top, Please

You are having a business meeting at a restaurant with one or more other guests. What table do you select? "I always choose a comfortable booth," you say. Wrong choice!

Booths are great, perhaps intimate if you are eating out with your spouse. Yet they are not best for business discussions. Always choose a four top (that's a single table with four sides and four chairs, for those of you who didn't do time in the food service business).

Why? Because four tops allow for more space to spread out. Each individual can move their chair in, out, or a bit to the side. Four tops allow for more individual comfort. Comfortable people listen better.

Also, take the seat with as little distraction behind you as possible. This is usually with your back to the wall. (This is not for the same reason the Mafia godfather chooses this seat!) The last thing you want is your customer or business contact being distracted by other people, tables, maître d', or servers moving behind you.

With a four top, you are more likely, if you planned well, to be diagonal to your colleague, guest, or customer. This avoids the across-the-table, competitive seating a booth induces. (Or in the worst case, sitting next to someone in a booth, which forces you and them to awkwardly turn your bodies to see the other.) Round tables are best for five or more people, but a four top sets you up for good, comfortable, and focused business conversations.

LESSON 132
Keeping Up Appearances

Nothing should distract from a patient's perception of quality and attentive care. That's why we insist on no food being visible to patients, anytime, anywhere (except in private offices). This doesn't mean our staff can't have drinks, but it does mean that those drinks must be only in approved K2 (two Kegarises—our businesses collectively—or K2) containers. Reasonably speaking, we can't allow patients to have our coffee cups (from our reception bar) and not allow staff to drink, yet we mostly discourage those coffee cups in favor of a Cool Springs EyeCare mug or thermos. No Dasani water bottles or mugs with other writing or labels allowed.

Depending on my or our manager's mood, we may just remind the employee and move the offensive drink to a nonvisible area. If it's a repeat offender, we have no problem emptying the drink and throwing out the bottle or food. We've found that when a person leaves food out and returns to find their food gone (and perhaps in the trash), they seem to get it from then on! Some people respond to a stick more than a carrot, and though we try to carry lots of carrots, the stick is always with us too!

As Dr. Don Berwick says, "Complex systems require simple rules"—and patient care *is* a complex system. Here's a simple rule: no food or drink except in approved containers when visible to patients. If Rudy Giuliani was successful in cleaning up a huge city like New York by eliminating seemingly small nuisances, like nonrequested window washers, and enforcing the stopping of petty crime as a way to discourage misbehavior and increase the impression of quality, safety, and image for the city, we can do the same in our little offices.

LESSON 133
Where to Smoke 'Em If You Have to Have 'Em

We wish you wouldn't smoke, yet some of you do. It's not our place to judge, yet we are the judge of our office. Therefore, we insist on three basic rules: First, no extra breaks. Smoking is allowed only before or after work or during lunch breaks. Second, smoking is allowed only in designated areas at certain distances that are behind the offices and not visible to patients. Third, smokers can't have any residual smoking smell on their person as perceived by us (if we can smell it, patients can too). We are a healthcare practice, and the smell of smoke or any other noxious odor is incompatible with the patients' perception of our delivery of a great patient-care experience.

LESSON 134
No Front Door Entrance or Exit for Us

We greet patients and guests at the front door—the focus is on them. So we try to design each of our offices so that the staff and doctors enter by side or back doors. We take a lesson from Disney: when we enter the office, we are on stage. We don't want patients seeing us come or go in front of them, unless we are available to take care of them.

This rule is important, but, of course, it's trumped by staff safety concerns.

LESSON 135
Office Design and NeverLost

An underestimated detail inherently important in every office is routing and signage. The staff knows where to find the sports vision gym, the optical department, the bathroom, and the checkout area, but the patient does not. Before GPS on everyone's phone and in every car, Hertz came out with NeverLost as an in-car value-added service for directions. I've always loved the name, and our office has adopted that goal for each of our patients: never lost.

Satisfy these two requirements, and you are well on your way to making it easy for your patients to find their way:

1. Imagine you are a new patient. Enter the front door and evaluate what signage you see. Is it friendly? Is it helpful and directional?

2. Look at your optical—how things are presented visually. With the average attention span shortening, people want to be directed quicker. Jonathan Smith from Luxottica commented at a meeting that patients and customers should be able to identify four brands within three seconds. Try this at your office and see how you do.

Beautiful office space.

Feels like I'm going to see friends instead of doctors.

Definitely a prime example of how people and businesses should exist.

CONCLUSION
Putting It All Together

This book is a quest to communicate the important things that we and everyone in our practice try to deliver every day. We are passionate about creating a great patient experience and about helping other doctors who want to create the same outstanding experience for their patients. It is really a guidebook for creating that experience in the doctor's office.

The short lessons represent easily implementable ideas—but if you are reading this as a patient, every idea may not be practiced. Start noticing when simple courtesies are provided, when personal relationships with your doctor and care team develop, and how they seem to value you in healthcare delivery. We have all experienced good and poor doctor office visits, some because of a staff member misstep, others because the leadership of the clinic or organization just doesn't care or is focused on other goals. In those settings, the doctors or leaders are not intentional about delivering consistently personalized care; rather, they just expect the experience to miraculously happen. The more you raise your expectation as a patient, the more you are raising the bar for better healthcare service. Reward those that deliver and practice it with your continued allegiance. Doctor-patient relationships should be generative—growing and strengthening over time.

> The more you raise your expectation as a patient, the more you are raising the bar for better health-care service. Reward those that deliver and practice it with your continued allegiance.

If you are a practitioner, you are likely to possess some aspects of great service that you are already proud of in your office. Use the lessons here to add to your repertoire of good service practices, and challenge yourself and your staff to listen better, respect more, and continuously improve. Do not attempt to mimic and implement them all at once; focus on a vital few.

An interesting thing happens as you focus and deepen the level of service by implementing some of these lessons. You'll start to see a service mentality become established in your doctor office and woven into the culture of your business. This leads to a reevaluation of processes and their impact on the patient experience. You start hiring and retaining staff who embrace the belief in superior service, and patients start to recognize and appreciate this. It leads to a differentiation between your practice and other healthcare practices, where your office starts to stand out as something different, unique, and better.

When this happens, patients talk and start to send their friends. You'll begin to build a loyal following and start to ask, "How do we know our patients are happy and our staff understands, is engaged, and growing?" And, importantly, you begin to focus on how to improve the clinical, operational, and developmental aspects of your business.

The road to achievement is not linear. You'll have many wins, brief periods of doubt, and a few anxious times feeling overwhelmed. Most importantly, you'll have fun and enjoy the excellent care you are providing, the happiness of your patients, the thanks expressed, the trust instilled, and the reputation you develop.

As both patients and doctors, you will find yourself noticing good, great, and poor service in many of the businesses you frequent. Your expectation for the care you desire and the care you as a patient deserve begins to grow. Rather than sitting and bemoaning the frustrations and burdens of the healthcare system, you'll both acknowledge their presence yet work to overcome the complexities and find ways to survive, thrive, and relentlessly improve by keeping an eye on care and the overall experience.

Congratulations! As a doctor, you haven't arrived yet, but you are well on your way to distinguishing yourself as a practitioner and business. And, one by one, we can work together, both patients and doctors, to increase the level of expectation for a better patient experience in each healthcare encounter.

I drive over an hour to come to this business, and it's well worth it.

I went there with an eye injury. Their first concern was getting me comfortable, even before asking for insurance. In this day and age, you cannot get anywhere without first doing the paperwork. Their first concern was me, which was greatly appreciated.

It's not often one finds a doctor willing to take such a personal interest in my eye health.

ACKNOWLEDGMENTS

In addition to the very special people mentioned earlier in this book and the influence they have had in shaping any of our mindset, growth, and success, there are many others, too numerous to list and thank. Below are a few people who have positively influenced or shaped us and our business thoughts through the sharing of their personal beliefs, methods, and expertise:

Dr. Paul Ajamian

Dr. Jim Marbourg

Dr. Kevin Alexander

Dr. John Amos

Dr. Jim McClendon

Dr. Arol Augsburger

Cindy McLaughlin

Dr. Jimmy Bartlett

Dr. Mark Murray

Dr. Don Berwick

Paige Pantall

Maureen Bisognano, RN

Dr. Todd Pfeil

Dr. Mike Polasky

Denice Boyers

Dr. Randy Reichle

Lucy Carter, CPA

Dr. Lou Catania

Dr. Michael Schuster

Bob Sircy

Jodi Strock

Dr. Scott Edmonds

Kay Swango

Dr. Gary Gerber

Marjorie Godfrey, RN

Larry Thomas

Scott Tilton

Dr. Steve Tuck

Katie Johnson

Dr. Fred Wallace

Dr. Chuck Kilo

David Crabtree

Dr. Doyle Leslie

Tom Lewis

Dr. David Talley

Dr. David Brown

APPENDIX

References and Recommended Reading

The Goal, Eliyahu M. Goldratt

The New One Minute Manager, Spencer Johnson, MD, and Kenneth Blanchard, PhD

The Leadership Challenge, James M. Kouzes and Barry Z. Posner

Thriving on Chaos, Tom Peters

The Discipline of Market Leaders, Michael Treacy and Fred Wiersema

The Service Edge: 101 Companies that Profit from Customer Care, Ron Zemke

Built to Last, Jim Collins

The Ultimate Marketing Plan, Dan S. Kennedy

Guerilla Marketing, Jay Conrad Levinson

The 22 Immutable Laws of Marketing, Al Ries and Jack Trout

Focus, Al Ries

See You at the Top, Zig Ziglar

Great Leaders Have No Rules, Kevin Kruse

The New Gold Standard, Joseph A. Michelli

Swim with the Sharks without Being Eaten Alive, Harvey Mackay

Mastering the Rockefeller Habits, Verne Harnish

Scaling Up, Verne Harnish

Customers for Life, Carl Sewell and Paul B. Brown

Confessions of the Pricing Man, Hermann Simon

Good to Great, Jim Collins

1001 Ways to Reward Employees, Bob Nelson

Curing Healthcare, Donald M. Berwick, A. Blanton Godfrey, and Jane Roessner

Escape Fire, Donald M. Berwick

The Machine That Changed the World, James P. Womack, Daniel T. Jones, and Daniel Roos

The Great Game of Business, Jack Stack

Open-Book Management, John Case

Zapp: The Lightning of Empowerment, William C. Byham

The Customer Connection, John Guaspari

Visionary Business, Marc Allen

The Starbucks Experience, Joseph Michelli

Nuts!, Kevin and Jackie Freiberg

If Disney Ran Your Hospital, Fred Lee

Straight Talk for Startups, Randy Komisar and Jantoon Reigersman

Above the Line, Urban Meyer

The E-Myth Revisited, Michael E. Gerber

The Advantage, Patrick Lencioni

The Experience Economy, B. Joseph Pine II

Delivering Knock Your Socks Off Service, Kristin Anderson and Ron Zemke

The 4 Disciplines of Execution, Chris McChesney, Sean Covey, and Jim Huling

Beyond IBM, Lou Mobley and Kate McKeown

Additional Recommended Resources

Institute for Healthcare Improvement, Boston, Massachusetts, www.ihi.org

The Tiger Institute for Cooperative Learning, Franklin, Tennessee, www.thetigerinstitute.com

Dartmouth Institute for Health Policy and Clinical Practice, Hanover, New Hampshire, www.clinicalmicrosystem.org

National Institute of Standards and Technology, Malcolm Baldrige National Quality Award and Performance Excellence Program, Washington, DC, www.nist.gov

CONTACT INFORMATION

Dr. Jeff Kegarise

The Center for Professional Development Inc.

620 Burghley Lane

Franklin, TN 37064

www.drjeffkegarise.com

Dr. Susan Kegarise

The Center for Professional Development Inc.

620 Burghley Lane

Franklin, TN 37064

www.drsusanandjeffkegarise.com

Cool Springs EyeCare

3252 Aspen Grove Drive

Franklin, TN 37067

(615) 771-7555

www.coolspringseyecare.com

Donelson EyeCare

2378 Lebanon Pike

Nashville, TN 37214

(615) 889-0147

www.donelsoneyecare.com

The Tiger Institute for Cooperative Learning

3252 Aspen Grove Drive, Suite 12

Franklin, TN 37067

(615) 419-4250

www.thetigerinstitute.com

drkegarise@thetigerinstitute.com

Performance Vision Therapy

3252 Aspen Grove Drive, Suite 12

Franklin, TN 37067

(615) 905-4668

www.performancevt.net

ABOUT THE AUTHORS

Dr. Jeff's Professional Journey

Optometry is a wonderful profession, and I continue to have a fulfilling career. I had a great foundational education at The Ohio State University College of Optometry, followed by a residency at the University of Alabama at Birmingham. It was there I was taught to *manage* patients, not just detect eye problems.

Starting at Austin Eye Associates/Texan Eye Center, I was charged with providing clinical care and building referrals from area optometrists. I enjoyed my working relationship with Dr. Doyle Leslie and learned invaluable early management lessons. I also learned that my dedication to encouraging doctors to refer patients to us for secondary eye care was always going to conflict with the owner's belief that we also needed to market directly to patients. This meant that we were competing for patients from the very doctors we were encouraging referrals from. Because his wife was the marketing director, I was always going to be the second runner up in a three-person race! It taught me the strength of having a single clear strategic focus.

I sought that focus in eye disease specialty referral centers. I was recruited to start a new center for Omega Health Systems in Birmingham, Alabama. Because I started before the center was opened (or had a definite location, for that matter), I spent time visiting area doctors, building rapport, listening to their needs, and envisioning the type of service-dedicated business I wanted to build. Thanks to strong support from the community of eye doctors the center grew very well and fast. I was a pretty young optometrist (thirty years old) running a multimillion-dollar practice. I thank God but also the CEO of the company, who gave me leniency, and the advisory board of optometrists, who gave me support, and shared their wisdom. I needed all three.

Within three years, that same CEO asked me if I would consider moving to Nashville to take over a struggling eye disease center. It was failing to the tune of over a million-dollar loss on barely two million dollars of top-line revenue. I was faced with a dilemma: stay in Birmingham and continue to grow what was becoming a lucrative business, or, to paraphrase Lebron James, "Take my talents to Nashville!" I chose the challenge. With Susan and three kids in tow, we moved to Music City, not knowing anyone.

What I encountered at VisionAmerica in Nashville was a defeated group of doctors, staff, and referring doctors. There was a culture of complaining and accepting their losses as circumstances beyond their control. There was no leadership with a vision, plan, or belief. VisionAmerica gave me experience in accomplishing a turnaround, both financially and culturally. It wasn't without challenges, as things would get worse before they got better.

The first challenge: The CEO decided to keep the previous director that I was replacing and have him report to me. So the guy I replaced now reported to me and there would not be any undermining? Yeah, right! In any business the leaders and staff must be aligned and believe in what can be. That means there cannot be any inner alliances detracting from the main mission. We ultimately built a strong belief in what could be and the positive "we're moving forward" overcame the negative "can't be done." I stayed, the previous guy left, and then we really took off.

The second challenge: We had a small surgical center in the office. The day I arrived, one of our patients had a serious health complication during cataract surgery. I had to respond, and we had to recover with the patient and the referring doctor. I pledged we would build quality systems into each of our patient and surgical processes.

The third challenge: 25 percent of our top-line revenue came from one optometry office in rural Tennessee. The doctor was one of the founders of the VisionAmerica concept and a well-respected businessman. We had a satellite in his office, and he was charging us a rent that was impractical for us to afford. I determined we needed to talk and come to a compromise, for the benefit of the center. Win-win was my goal, yet we could not agree to a compromise. He would not budge. He essentially said, "You can't do without me," and "You'd be a fool to lose our support, as it's the only thing keeping your center afloat." He had underestimated my resolve and we parted ways. I wanted congruency around the new vision, and we found other supporters that more than made up for our revenue loss from his referrals.

At VisionAmerica, we put into practice concepts that had worked at the previous center locations: a focus on service, people, teamwork, referring doctors, and internal systems. Thanks to my dad's influence, I added a framework for organizational success based on the Malcolm Baldrige National Quality Award. It became our goal to win a Baldrige. I was also fortunate to have a great partner in business, as ophthalmologist Daniel Bregman was recruited to our center. Daniel epitomized the "service first" responsiveness to referring doctors and worked his tail off to build optometric support for our center. He deserves all the success he has had because he certainly put in the work.

We ultimately became the largest of the Omega referral centers, growing from a staff of six members to seventy-plus and from two locations of business to fourteen. Many talented staff grew into positions of authority, exceeding their previous ambitions. We developed a great team and received national and international recognition for service and business methods in not just eye care, but rather, healthcare. And we had a lot of fun. Oh yeah, we also made a lot of money for the company! Turning around a distressed company and making it successful was rewarding.

Eventually, a very successful optometrist in the area wanted to retire or slowly phase out, as he had become burned out. I realized it was the right time for me (and Susan) and my career, as well as the right location and partner doctor. His practice was medium in size and mostly focused on vision care. With my eye healthcare and disease background, we began transitioning the practice to provide comprehensive eye health and vision care. Thus, my third practice experience was turning an already successful, albeit limited focus business, into a broader scope.

Once again, we started with service as the foundation. Change is not easy, and indeed, we had transitions in staff, including the partner doctor. But I learned that sometimes, the people that get you to one point in your business evolution may not be the same people to take you to the next level. I continued to focus on cultivating leaders to expand their capabilities to take on more responsibility when the time came. Today, I am surrounded by a great team, and we are laser focused on service and patient relationships. We have built a great organization with an outstanding reputation. And yet, we have only scratched the surface of what we can become.

Susan and I have done a lot right in our careers in management. We have also stumbled and screwed up (more my screwups than hers). We try to be open with staff and doctors about what we do and how we try to do it. We try a lot of things, keep what works, and throw out what doesn't. There are foundational service elements and behaviors we have instilled, taught, demonstrated, and insisted upon in caregivers and staff. To make those go from oral history to written canon, we started writing our K2 service manual. The service manual ultimately expanded to become this book as an effort to help other doctors.

We have started de novo practices, rescued failing businesses and taken successful practices to a "next level" of performance. We have learned from so many people and have tried to acknowledge them wherever we could in these teachings. Many lessons are original, while others were read about, observed, or taught to us by someone. All have been implemented in our businesses. We are open to theory but only if it results in practical improvements. Every healthcare practice (or any business) faces different circumstances and challenges. They always seem to be unique. Yet, they inevitably require some fundamental knowledge or concepts that, if consistently applied, help solve even the most vexing of issues. We believe that a commitment to ideal service is a foundational principle. It is because our people believe, demonstrate, and deliver service every day that we succeed. The starting point is for your employees to know and act on these ideal service principles. As eye doctors, we feel a focus should be evident in every aspect of healthcare. That's a vision we want everyone to embrace.

Dr. Susan's Professional Journey

I wanted to be an optometrist ever since sitting in my eye doctor's chair as a child in elementary school. The clicking and flipping of the dials was melodic and mesmerizing. I even malingered—wanting so much to wear glasses that I feigned blurry vision, even when the eye chart was clear. My doctor caught on!

Attending The Ohio State University fulfilled my goals for undergraduate and professional studies. (I still do and always will bleed scarlet and gray!) Although I had always lived in Ohio, the progressive training in eye healthcare and disease management, combined with a potent faculty at the University of Alabama at Birmingham, School of Optometry, was compelling enough to get me to move elsewhere. Led by Dr John Amos, with frequent interactions with the likes of Drs. Jimmy Bartlett, Larry Alexander, Leo Semes, and others, the residency program gave me the clinical confidence I desired.

Optometry and ophthalmology were competitively antagonistic in those days. I was fortunate to join Dr. Michael Callahan, an ophthalmologist who needed someone to develop a contact lens program in his office. Though the two eye professions may fight on a legislative and political landscape, when doctors work together, mutual respect commonly develops. I learned a lot from Mike, and I think he learned that optometry and ophthalmology could work together cooperatively for the betterment of patient care. With Jeff and I married, we had the dilemma facing many dual professional couples: Whose career do we follow? We chose Jeff's, and off to Austin, Texas, we went. I still remember Dr. Doyle Leslie during Jeff's prestart dinner saying to me, "Since you are an optometrist too, I'd rather have you working for me than against me!" I joined Austin

Eye Associates (later, Texan Eye Center) working in the main office and spearheading a rural practice in Elgin, Texas. Jeff and I shared an office at Dr. Leslie's practice that was so small our chairs bumped into each other if we backed away from our respective desks. Conversations about eyes have never overwhelmed our marriage. We both love eye care and patient care and working together has always been (and still is!) fun.

When moving back to Birmingham, I wanted to find or start a private practice. It was a balance with our then-growing three-child family to say the least. Drs. Cathie Amos and Bryan Boozer each added me on as a part-time provider. In their practices I became better exposed to real primary care optometry and was fortunate to observe two doctors who excelled in patient care and business management. These two lifelong friends taught me so many things that would be helpful in my next optometric journey.

Once we moved to Nashville, it gave me the chance to pursue the ultimate goal of having my own optometry practice. I bought a practice from a doctor who decided he wanted to become a priest. The practice was so small that I thought it was perfect. When I say small, I mean eight inches of charts, eight hundred square feet, and one employee small. It was a chance to implement my own patient care beliefs and systems and to stamp my identity on the community of Donelson, Tennessee.

When you own your own business and you are the primary caregiver, it is difficult to escape the responsibilities. Indeed, the needs of patients, staff, and the business never stop and certainly do not respect an eight-to-five schedule. The practice is always on your mind. To the extent that you care—and I do love my patients, staff, and the Donelson community—it's work that you just do, not thinking of the hours you put in or the pay you receive. When I remember back to where the practice was and then look at where it is now—two expansion moves, four doctors, and a rotating surgeon on staff—I do swell a little with pride!

I enjoy so many of the relationships and friendships that have developed over the time the practice has grown. I have shared in the visual improvement of thousands of people, celebrated their wins, commiserated during their complications. Eye healthcare and vision improvement is what I do, yet I am in the business of building, fostering, and maintaining relationships with our patients. Jeff and I both talk to patients about their lives, hopes, dreams, frustrations, and successes. Our job is to know them so well that we can find the best methods of protection, correction, and enhancement of their vision and then help them fulfill their needs and dreams.

Growth in a business or medical practice is a testament to success in building trust. I still think the lessons in this book are mostly obvious and easily implemented. Success comes not from the lessons contained herein but from constantly expecting them to be followed—reminding, teaching, and maintaining them as standards. The key to success is what's called management. As Jeff's dad, Ron, likes to point out, "If management was so easy, there wouldn't be so many people writing books about it." Leading and managing a business takes work—often arduous in the moment yet rewarding in the long run … and fun!

In this season of our careers, we both may be seeing patients on fewer days, yet the practices are still our babies. This book is aimed at helping doctors deliver and nurture their own babies and at helping patient's amp up their expectations—demanding the highly responsive and respectful care they deserve. It's been a great optometric journey for us so far. Helping others accomplish their own joy in the journey and continuing to advocate for improved healthcare is what excites us now. Here is hoping that we can help you enjoy your work and life as much as we enjoy ours.

Drs. Jeff Kegarise and Susan Kegarise

Board-Certified Optometrists

Diplomats, American Board of Optometry

Owners:

> Cool Springs EyeCare
>
> Donelson EyeCare
>
> Performance Vision Therapy
>
> The Competitive Edge – Sports Vision
>
> The Tiger Institute for Cooperative Learning
>
> Center for Professional Development
>
> And future eye-care and other businesses

Franklin and Nashville, Tennessee

I could go somewhere else, but the service I get from this location is amazing.

I was greeted with many smiles and felt comfortable the whole time.

Wouldn't go anywhere else.

I'd give ten stars if I could.

Printed in the USA
CPSIA information can be obtained
at www.ICGtesting.com
JSHW012021140824
68134JS00033B/2808